The story of
An Icon

The full history, tradition and spirituality of the popular icon of Our Mother of Perpetual Help

The story of
An Icon

The full history, tradition and spirituality of the popular icon of Our Mother of Perpetual Help

Fabriciano Ferrero, C.Ss.R.

A Redemptorist Publication

Published by **Redemptorist Publications**
A Registered Charity limited by guarantee. Registered in England 3261721

First published in 1994 in Spanish under the title SANTA MARIA DEL
PERPETUO SOCORRO Un icono de la Santa Madre de Dios 'Virgen de La
Passion' con el Presagio de la Pasion gloriosa de Cristo, PS Editorial, Madrid,

English translation by: First Edition Translations Cambridge England
Editor: Michael McGreevy, C.Ss.R.
Design: Rosemarie Pink

Copyright © 2001 Redemptorist Publications

This edition printed March 2001
Reprinted November 2001

ISBN 0 85231 219 9

Printed by Estudios Gráficos Zure, Spain

Alphonsus House Chawton Hampshire GU34 3HQ
Telephone 01420 88222   Fax 01420 88805
rp@ShineOnline.net   www.ShineOnline.net

CONTENTS

Christian iconography
expresses in images
the same Gospel message
that Scripture communicates by words.
Image and Word illuminate each other.

Catechism of the Catholic Church no. 1160

THE AUTHOR'S PREFACE TO THE ORIGINAL EDITION

The icon of Our Mother of Perpetual Help is one of the most popular representations of the Virgin Mary. As may often happen with artistic treasures with which we are familiar, we can lose sight of its aesthetic and cultural significance. This icon was valued simply as an image for devotional veneration. It has taken specialists, antiquarians and art experts, to remind us that the original is an authentic icon of the Mother of God from the series known as "Virgins of the Passion".

Many people pray before this image of the Virgin, transfixed by the gaze through which she speaks to her followers. However, relatively few are able to appreciate the theology contained within the work and the mystery it holds. This is because they do not know how to read the icon and, still less, how to allow themselves to be read by it. Yet it would be difficult to find another image that has as much to tell us about the Mother of God as this icon of the Virgin of the Passion. To make this discovery we need an appropriate and accurate introduction that will help us to understand the icon's symbols and to penetrate its theological significance. In this way the icon can also become a book of Christian prayer and a place of contemplation that brings us before the mystery of the Redemption.

In presenting this work I should like to express my gratitude to all those who helped to make it possible. I should like to give a special mention to the Redemptorist Province of Madrid and to its publishing house, Editorial El Perpetuo Socorro. I should also like to thank the General Curia of the Congregation of the Most Holy Redeemer, for the use of their historical archive and the shrine of Our Mother of Perpetual Help in Rome for the facilities they made available to me for my research. I should also like to mention those most closely involved in the immediate preparation of the materials: Dr Giorgio Vasari, Fr Carlos Pereira, Fr Antonio Marrazzo, Fr Rafael Gonzalez and Fr Jose Morales. Frs Jose Maria Lorca and Vidal Ayala were responsible for the design and followed the publishing process at every stage to ensure the work produced would be both educational and attractive. I remember them all with gratitude.

Fabriciano Ferrero, C.Ss.R.

Note to the English edition: we have taken account of the 1994 restoration of the icon and its shrine and a description of this work is included here (p.101).

The icon of Our Mother of Perpetual Help in Sant' Alfonso Church, Rome. The newly restored icon in the remodelled sanctuary was solemnly blessed on 27 June 1995.

INTRODUCTION

THE SIGNIFICANCE OF THE THEME AND THE APPROACH ADOPTED IN THIS STUDY

This is the first authenticated copy of the icon of Our Mother of Perpetual Help to leave Rome in 1866. It is enshrined in the Redemptorist community Oratory, Bishop Eton Monastery, Liverpool, England.

1. THE ICON REVIVAL

"If someone asks you to demonstrate your faith to them,
bring them to a church and place them before the sacred icons."
St. John Damascene

U ntil little more than half a century ago, icons, the supreme example of the artistic and religious expression of eastern Christianity, were almost completely unknown in western culture. Today, however, they are emerging as part of humanity's spiritual heritage and worthy of the greatest attention.

It is not surprising then that icons should have become much sought after in the art world and occupy a place of honour in antique shops and the homes of wealthy collectors. So much so that, between 1980 and the end of 1992, "twenty-seven million icons were illegally exported from Russia", according to the Moscow News Agency. As a result of this increasingly widespread and popular demand, there has been a considerable growth in copies and reproductions of icons, using a variety of different techniques to ensure their wide distribution.

Icons are also very much in vogue as one of the most characteristic expressions of symbolic images. Through them it is possible to discover a Christian experience of God, the fruit of the iconographer's faith, contemplation and prayer; a theology of revealed truths moulded into aesthetic forms; and a universe of symbols that leads us back to the local churches where they originated. This is why they are so greatly appreciated among representatives of culture, art and religion.

All of which has prepared the ground for icons to occupy the privileged place due to them in Christian prayer, worship, liturgy, spirituality, popular piety and the ecumenical concerns of the western church – a place that they had never lost in eastern churches.[1]

But for those who belong to a different culture from that represented in such images, icons are works of art that are not easy to understand or appreciate. As with all works of symbolic character, they require an authentic introduction. It is not possible, in a spontaneous way, to capture the message of which they are bearers and which they set out to convey. "A human being is a creature who creates symbols". And "a symbol does not signify: it evokes and focuses, reunites and concentrates, in an analogous way, a multiplicity of meanings that can not be reduced to a single meaning, nor even to several... The symbol depends on the mythical and ritual context with which it is associated."[2]

Thus, although at times it may have seemed to be so, the icon is neither an idol nor a charm, but a symbol. It resembles a "sacred page" which conveys a message of salvation to us. To grasp this message, we need to know how to "read" the page on which it is found and "to allow oneself to be read" by it. It is not by chance that the term "iconographer" – writer of images – is used for the individual called upon to paint such icons. And this being so, the person who contemplates these works of piety and art must be a "reader" of symbols.

But there is still something more. This sacred page has a very precise place in liturgical worship, popular religious belief and private piety "as an affective medium for knowing God, the Virgin and the saints" and bringing us into contact with them. However, it does not involve theoretical and abstract teaching. It is performed in a liturgical style, that is to say, directed at all the faculties of the human being, taking into account the spiritual experience and tradition of the Church, and expressing concisely the totality of a mystery or a festival. For this reason, icons will be really understood when the viewer contemplates them appropriately as symbols of invisible realities.[3]

2. THE ICON OF OUR MOTHER OF PERPETUAL HELP

The study, which we now present, is not concerned with icons in general. It is restricted to one of the Mother of God, belonging to the Virgin of the Passion type and named Our Mother of Perpetual Help.

Historical background

This icon is currently venerated in the church of the Most Holy Redeemer and Saint Alphonsus in Rome. But its pictorial style, just as its tradition and legend, lead us back to the iconographic school of Crete in the second half of the 14th century or at the beginning of the 15th century. From the end of this same century

(1480-1499) until the last years of the 18th century (1798-1799), it was venerated in the church of Saint Matthew in Merulana (Rome) with the Italian title of: Madonna di S. Matteo; Madonna, Madonna Santissima or Santa Maria, del Soccorso; and Madonna del Soccorso Perpetuo or del Perpetuo Soccorso, which were translated into Latin as: Sancta Maria de/a Succursu and Sancta Maria Succursus Perpetui or de Perpetuo Succursu, and which was rendered in English as: Mother of Perpetual Succour.

Following the destruction of St Matthew's church in 1799, the icon remained half-forgotten in the convent of Santa Maria in Posterula, in the same city of Rome.

On 26 April 1866, it was again placed on display for public veneration in the church of St Alphonsus where it remains today, under the title of Holy Mother of Perpetual Help, or, in Latin, Sancta Maria de Perpetuo Succursu. Hence the invocation: Mater de Perpetuo Succursu, ora pro nobis!, that was requested in the year 1916, was introduced into the Litany of Loreto.

This gave rise to a new Marian devotion, intimately related to the spirituality of Saint Alphonsus de Liguori (1696-1787) and to the Congregation of the Most Holy Redeemer which he founded in Scala, Salerno, Italy, 1732. The church in Rome in which the icon was displayed, belonged to this Congregation and had been consecrated on 3 May 1859.

The Basilica of Our Lady of Perpetual Help (Mission Church), Boston, USA, famous for its Golden Shrine and the people's great devotion.

Iconographic importance

The universal spread of this form of devotion, due in a large part, to the apostolic ministry of the Redemptorists, constitutes a socio-religious phenomenon of great interest in the history of iconography and popular religious belief. In fact, it enables us to see the evolution of the iconographic theme, represented in the icon, and the historical process that followed the devotion, adopting it as its own image.

Young Venezuelans. The association of Our Mother of Perpetual Help with Redemptorist missionaries has transformed it into the most popular icon in the western world.

It is true that, from an artistic point of view, the icon of Our Mother of Perpetual Help does not figure among the most famous. However, after one hundred and thirty-five years of being in the service of Christian piety in the Churches of the East and West, it has become one of the most popular. For precisely this reason, it is also one of those that has been most exposed to iconographic distortion. Without losing its fundamental symbolic elements, artists have adapted it to the aesthetics of each region, reducing it, in many cases, to a simple devotional image.

Link with Marian intercession and popular devotion to the Mother of God

In fact, although iconographically speaking, it belongs to the type known as the Virgin of the Passion, these days it is impossible to separate it from the Marian devotion to Our Mother of Perpetual Help. Its wide-reaching scope, as a religious symbol, can not yet override this ecclesiastical function that it has assumed since 1866. Other icons have their place in the iconostasis, or in the shrine from which they received their title and where we are invited to contemplate them. Nowadays, however, icons of the Virgin of the Passion are inseparable not so much from their shrines as from Marian devotion to Our Mother of Perpetual Help. The devotion and the icon form part of a socio-religious phenomenon that would be incomprehensible without one of them, or considered separately. In fact, it is common to refer to all the icons of this type as the Virgin of Perpetual Succour, instead of the Virgin of the Passion. For this reason, when we say: Our Mother of Perpetual Succour, we have to include the icon of the Virgin of the Passion and the Marian devotion that has appropriated it. Without the icon, the devotion would disappear. And by contrast, without the devotion, the icon would become a museum piece. And an icon in an art gallery is like a gem in a jeweller's shop: we can admire and contemplate it, perhaps better than in real life, but we will never be able to understand the social and aesthetic function for which it was created. The same is true of icons – they will only regain their original splendour when they again occupy the site for which they were painted. But the icon of Our Mother of Perpetual Succour has acquired its own context (added to those of the past) in the Marian devotion that it now symbolises. The sanctuary of Crete, in which it was so venerated as the Virgin of the Passion, has been replaced by altars to Our Mother of Perpetual Help that the devotion has created all over the world.

While other icons may be valuable in themselves, the icon of Our Mother of Perpetual Help is all the more valuable for the devotion aroused by its contemplation.

Devotional heritáge

In order better to understand the relationship between the icon and devotion, it is important to remember that the origins of the present devotion to Our Mother of Perpetual Help (Rome, 1866), included a Marian devotion, known as Madonna del Soccorso, with a very weak historical, iconographic, theological and devotional background. At that time, devotion to the Virgin of Succour, or to Our Mother of Succour, did not yet have any significance for Marian piety, apart from a few local sanctuaries.

The discovery of the devotion to and the icon of Saint Matthew, in the middle of the 19th century, and the establishment of its following in the Roman church of Saint Alphonsus, added to this minor historical heritage the power which at that time the Alphonsian and Redemptorist "Marian piety" held in the Christian world. This gave rise, in effect, to a new devotion, with all the elements that any "devotion" always assumes: a sanctuary, intercession, an iconographic expression, a hagiographic legend, certain anthropological and cultural values, certain "typical" forms of worship, of veneration and piety, and a theological explanation of all these elements.

The Arabic version of Our Mother of Perpetual Help. An example of the variety of interpretations, remaining faithful to its fundamental iconographic elements.

In its later evolution, the special devotion took precedence over the icon. Until very recent times, almost no allusion was made to the icon, except to explain the miraculous character of the image. And popular devotion to the icon concentrated, above all, on the practice of Marian piety and Christian devotion, based on traditional veneration of the images: associations, confraternities, archconfraternities, novenas, processions, perpetual intercession, home visiting, centres of charity and hospitality, and the like.

3. THE NATURE OF THIS STUDY

The historical documentation concerning all these aspects is very rich, and at least in part, has already been studied.[4] Nowadays, however, there is also a need to address the iconographic heritage of the devotion. In attempting this, we were aware that we could not limit ourselves to written sources and traditional historical forms. Popular devotion, linked to images directed towards prayer and of symbolic content, has certain anthropological, cultural, aesthetic, religious and liturgical dimensions that are difficult to capture, if one overlooks the iconographic documentation that accompanies them. This means that one of the most suitable techniques for realising this may be historical-anthropological exhibitions and illustrated publications, which include graphic documentation alongside the more traditional documents and studies.

This was the inspiration behind a book on Our Mother of Perpetual Help in which graphic documentation would be as valid and important as literary and bibliographic material.

A procession in Kingston, Jamaica.

In structuring the material we had been gathering and selecting for this purpose, we also noted how the iconographic themes of Marian devotion date back, in some way to the origins of Christian art, although it is not always easy to distinquish this in concrete forms observable in each kind of devotion. The continuity of fundamental symbolic elements may be eclipsed by the diversity of the variants accentuated in every element as a result of the unceasing artistic creativity of each epoch, style, school, region or artist. However, icons appear to be an exception to this process since they tend to remain very faithful to the iconographic archetype from which they are derived.

4. GENERAL STRUCTURE OF THE BOOK

Taking these criteria into account, we have divided our study into five chapters.

In the *first chapter*, we introduce the nature of the icon in general, the spiritual message of which it is the bearer and the function that it can have for prayer. We look at the practical demands that an approach to it, with this aim, presupposes, and the historical diversity that has to be taken into account.

In the *second chapter*, we study the Marian iconographic themes that appear to explain the symbolic elements and significance of icons, in general, and the Virgin of the Passion, in particular. In this way, the reader will be able to appreciate the transition from the symbolic images of paleo-christian iconography to the artistic symbolism of the Mother of God, that culminates in the *Hodegetria*. This resulted, from the 5th century onwards, in the face and hands of this iconographic model being transformed into the face and hands of the Mother of God. In the *Eleusa*, later icons and painting prior to the Renaissance, these were consecrated and respected, within their own variants and this, in fact, helps us to understand the significance of the *Virgin of the Passion*.

The *third chapter* is devoted to the iconographic theme of the *Virgin of the Passion*. Here we concentrate on aspects that will help us understand the specific example that we want to study. This will create a better appreciation of the elements inherited from the earlier archetypes and of the variants that have been in this new iconographic theme. We also pay particular attention to the Creto-Venetian School as it is to this school that the icon of Our Mother of Perpetual Help belongs.

The *fourth chapter* deals with what was the point of departure of our interest in the subject – the icon of Our Mother of Perpetual Help. Our interest here is, above all, in it as an icon of the type known as *Virgin of the Passion*. We will study its iconographic elements, something of the materials with which it is made, and its aesthetic structure. This chapter concludes with the remarkable historical provenance of this icon.

The *fifth chapter* invites us to re-read the icon of Our Mother of Perpetual Help. We look more closely at each element in the icon. It is in its contemplation that we discover the way it expresses the Gospel message of the good news of salvation in Christ Jesus.

The first appendix to the book presents the remarkable document from St Matthew's Church in Merulana which tells the early history of the icon. There are further notes on the illustrations. And, finally, we offer a list of Shrines of Our Mother of Perpetual Help around the world culled from the Inscriptiones CSsR 2000, Rome.

We hope that all these elements will help to create a better understanding of the message of the icon of Our Mother of Perpetual Help, above all, for those who make use of it, as a religious image of devotion and prayer.

Notes to the Introduction

[1] The Catechism of the Catholic Church, 1992, deals explicitly with the subject in all its constituent parts. The relevant paragraphs are as follows: Part I The profession of the Christian faith: the true body of Christ, nos. 476 and 477. Part II The celebration of the Christian mystery: How to celebrate the liturgy: the sacred images, nos. 1159-1162 and 1198. Part III The life in Christ: "Thou shalt not make for yourself a graven image", nos. 2129-2132 and 2141. Part IV Christian prayer: favourable places for prayer, and expressions of prayer: meditation, nos. 2691 and 2705. These texts deal with the resumption of the patristic tradition and the doctrine of the ecumenical councils of Nicea II, Trent and Vatican II. cf. no. 2132.

[2] R. Alleau: La scienza dei simboli (The science of symbols), Florence, 1983

[3] M. Donadeo: Iconos de la Madre de Dios (Icons of the Mother of God), Madrid, 1991.

[4] cf. Archivum Generale Historicum Redemptoristarum (AGHR), Rome: Sectio B. M. V. de Perpetuo Succursu (PS), VII, 10. For bibliographic information on the subject cf. F. Ferrero: Our Lady of Perpetual Help: bibliographic information and general chronology, in "Spicilegium Historicum C.Ss.R", 38 (1990), 455-502.

The church of St Alphonsus Liguori, "The Rock" Church, in St Louis, MO, USA. From this church the Perpetual Novena devotions spread across the world.

A POPE'S PRAYER

Oh Mother of Perpetual Help,
Holy Mother of the Redeemer,
magnificent sign of our hope,
we entreat you,
come to the aid of your people,
who long to rise again.
Give to all the joy
of approaching the third millennium
in conscious and active solidarity
with the poorest among us,
proclaiming in a new and valiant manner
the Gospel of your Son,
the foundation and summit
of all human co-existence,
in longing for a true,
fair and lasting peace.
Like the infant Jesus,
whom we admire in this venerated icon,
we too wish to clasp your right hand.
You have the power and the goodness
to help us
in every need and situation.
This is your hour!
Come to our aid
and be the refuge and the hope
of us all.
Amen.

John Paul II, 30 June 1991

CHAPTER I

A THEOLOGY AND HISTORY OF ICONS

1. NATURE AND MESSAGE OF ICONS

2. ATTITUDES AND REQUIREMENTS FOR THEIR CONTEMPLATION

3. HISTORICAL DEVELOPMENT
   a) Theological study of the Mother of God
   b) An overview of the development of art in the Roman Empire
   c) The Post-Byzantine School of Crete (1453-1669)

Notes to Chapter I

The Virgin of the Sign, with St Nicholas and St Blaise,
15ᵗʰ-16ᵗʰ century.

The image of Our Mother of Perpetual Help is an authentic icon. To understand and appreciate it fully, we need to remember the nature, the message, the socio-religious function and the historical development of this type of sacred representation.

1. NATURE AND MESSAGE OF ICONS

Icons are always "visible representations of supernatural things" (Dionysius the Areopagite) and are the bearers of a religious message that can only be discovered by approaching their contemplation in a particular way.

Image and sacred representation

The Greek word *eikón*, from which the current term in other languages derives, means image, figure, representation. In the history of art it is used as a technical term to describe a type of sacred image found in eastern churches. In these images, Christ, the Virgin and the saints are represented in accordance with very precise theological, aesthetic, technical and liturgical norms. Sometimes they appear individually, sometimes as part of scenes from the Bible, or of historical events, hagiographic legends, theological themes or liturgical celebrations.

Jesus, the supreme icon

Christians originally applied this term to the Word Incarnate. "He is the image (icon) of the invisible God, the firstborn of all creation; for in him all things in heaven and on earth were created" (Col 1:15-16). Through contemplation of him we are able to draw closer to the mystery of God and the mystery of creation.

But that is not all. Christ, the image and imprint of God in the first creation (Col 1:15, Heb 1:3), came to restore to fallen humanity, by means of a new creation won for us through his death (2 Cor 5:17), the splendour of that divine image lost through sin (Gen 1:26; 3:22-24; Rom 5:12). And he does this by imprinting on humanity a yet more splendid image – that of the children of God.

In this way Jesus Christ, truly God and truly man, through whose humanity divinity was revealed, is the supreme icon. Through his contemplation we discover the image of God the Father who is in heaven and our own condition as children of God. Both humans and the whole of creation are therefore called upon to reflect this mystery and the glory they will one day enjoy in the Resurrection. He is the "gateway" through which we enter the kingdom of heaven.

All icons embody a mysterious presence …

The iconographer "writes" the icons he produces from his faith and from his contemplation of the multiform presence of God. Through these icons, through their images and colours, he seeks to present to other believers something of this mysterious world he has discovered and that he is endeavouring to understand more fully.

Icon of the Mandilion or the Holy Face of Christ. Christ is the foremost and fundamental "image of the invisible God" (Colossians 1:15).

Hence the theological significance of icons. Through the beauty of their images they reflect the mystery of God as revealed in Christ, in the Mother of God, in the saints and in creation. But in these images, as in the Scriptures, there is not simply the "aesthetic element" but the mysterious presence of what they represent. "The icon, in fact, is a kind of exhortation: what a book is to those who can read, the icon is to those who can not; what the word is to our sense of hearing, the icon is to our sense of sight – it is through the mind, however, that we make sense of this (what these two things mean)". (St John Damascene, *De Imaginibus*)[1]

For eastern Christians, from the ninth century onwards in particular, icons became something more than a simple reminder of significant events or individuals in the history of salvation. They provide a non-rational presence of what is represented, referring us to something that can only be discovered, represented and contemplated through the eyes of faith, even in the case of inanimate objects.[2] In some way they give presence to what they represent, thus becoming authentic holy objects: "the symbol and the site of the divine presence, the temple in which that which is mysteriously represented, becomes mysteriously present, drawing closer to people to remind us that we too have been made in God's image, that we share in his divine nature and that therefore we too are 'icons' of God".[3] It is for this reason that in eastern churches the icon is venerated alongside the Word of God, as a "sacred page" whose "reading" should culminate in contemplation, in prayer and commitment.

In fact, "the icon began as a reminder, a representation, image or portrait of individuals who, having borne witness to Christ through their life (confirmed in some instances by their martyrdom), were worthy of being commemorated." In the 6th century, however, the icon became something more. As with relics, it was itself transformed into an object of devotion and began to be venerated in churches, monasteries, palaces and even in the home, not simply as the commemoration of an event or an individual, but also as embodying a presence and a mysterious power, that gave it a mystical and thaumaturgic value.[4] This power was one of the arguments put forward at the Second Council of Nicea (in 787) to justify the veneration of sacred images by the faithful.[5]

The "Triumph of Orthodoxy" icon. This represents the exaltation of icons, placing them alongside the Word of God.

This way of thinking about icons also led to the adoption of a practice customary with judges in the Roman courts. "They would meet in a room in which a portrait took the place of the emperor or sovereign in whose name they would pass judgement. In the same way, icons of Christ or of the Mother of God came to indicate their presence in the place where they were displayed. It is easy to imagine the effect that this concept might have on the religious, civil, public and private life of the Byzantine peoples, as well as the influence it was naturally bound to have on the form taken by works of art (and painting in particular) and on the images themselves in general".[6]

In effect, "the presence of a sacred element in every image, encouraged the use of a grave and solemn style, a priestly approach in the general attitude and gestures, and a more or less explicit rejection of the imitative modelling of bodies and objects and of the space and movement contained therein".[7] "An image intended for devotion cannot be conceived in the same way as a painting whose sole purpose it to provide aesthetic pleasure. Veneration demands a priestly, rhythmical composition stripped down to its essential elements, a composition that is clear and intelligible; it requires figures who address themselves to the viewer in an almost priestly attitude and gesture; it demands colours that give the impression of supernatural light. Yet at the same time an icon must remain different from an idol: an image intended to be an object of veneration must not be confused with an image seen as an object of adoration. In contrast with the exaggerated, aggressive realism of the idol, the Byzantine icon simply evokes, suggests, symbolises. It is not in essence an object but a dogma expressed through an image".[8]

The icon as the product of a contemplative attitude

To capture the mystery that the icon is called upon to reflect, the iconographer would create his work in an atmosphere of fasting and prayer, conscious always of the contemplative purpose to which it would be put by those who used it in many different circumstances in life. The religious images of Christian antiquity therefore reflect both the faith and piety of their creator as well as that of the Christian people.

People at prayer in the Church of St Alphonsus in Tafara, Harare, Zimbabwe. The icon, to the right of the sanctuary (above) and in the Community Chapel in Tafara, is an invitation to contemplate in prayer the mystery of God's redeeming love.

Icons can also be considered as symbolic images of an artistic and theological nature which both refer to and recall far more than they represent. In these images the form and meaning of the symbol have been sublimated by the power of the sacred objects while, at the same time they acquire aesthetic and psycho-religious qualities capable of influencing those who contemplate them. The icon, like the word of God, invites us to contemplate the mystery contained within and to allow ourselves to be penetrated by it – by the splendour, luminosity and glory of the invisible that can penetrate the deepest corners of the soul.

These qualities in icons are what make them "images of the invisible", the bearers of a spiritual message and highly accessible to contemplation. When we place ourselves before them in an appropriate manner, they begin gradually to arouse in us an attitude of prayer. The ideal place for this is a

Religious celebrations like this one at the Novena Church, Singapore, help to highlight the significance of icons for prayer.

space set aside for this fundamental spiritual and devotional need.

The Bible of the Christian people and sacred page for "lectio divina"

It has been said that the stained glass windows of medieval cathedrals and the iconography of ancient places of worship in general constituted "the people's Bible". Pursuing this image, we could say that icons are "pages of the book in which God speaks to people", as the Church Fathers referred to the Holy Scripture.[9] Or, if we prefer, gateways (Christ is seen as a gateway) and windows opening on to the mystery of God and the invisible world, through which we are able to enter this world and contemplate it and which simultaneously project on to us the brilliance of the divinity. These images are simple and easy, yet also rich and deep in content, like the words of the Bible. And for this reason, if we wish to understand them, we must study them and seek out their deeper meaning in the same way as we do with biblical texts, the starting point of the "lectio divina".[10]

The icon as a theme for prayer

Icons are written by the iconographer in the midst of contemplation, meditation and prayer and this is also how they must be read. In reading such works we seek to understand the deep significance and the concealed message they contain, in order to improve still further our enjoyment and experience of them.

However, it requires tranquillity and time to read the "sacred page" and to be read by it – that is to say, to contemplate the icon and to allow ourselves to be penetrated by the gaze of those represented or by the mystery it expresses. Silence, both external and internal, and an atmosphere of private and communal prayer and brotherly dialogue provide the best environment in which to achieve this. Together these elements will give rise to prayer, the final attitude of the believer before an icon. The forms this prayer can take range from pure contemplation and humble supplication, through praise and practical commitment, to profound adoration and filial gratitude.[11]

2. ATTITUDES AND REQUIREMENTS FOR THEIR CONTEMPLATION

We shall now go on to say something of the practical requirements for presenting an icon as an object of contemplation and prayer. These derive from the symbolic and sacred nature of the image and from the religious message that it carries. The most important considerations are described below.

Fidelity to the original model

It is not enough for the image simply to retain its symbolic content. To express this fully it must also remain as faithful as possible to the aesthetic language of the icon and be either a genuine icon or a faithful copy of one – because not all interpretations and reproductions, however religious or artistic they may be, contain the sacred power of the genuine article.

Aesthetic and religious setting

However, having an authentic icon is not sufficient in itself. It is possible to have such an image but not to be in a position to transform it into an object or theme of contemplation and prayer. While an icon is a sacred object with its own aesthetics, a religious message to convey and a spiritual function to fulfil, the question of where, when, how, in what light and in what architectural or sound environment it is displayed is not without importance. Lamps, candles, incense, music, space, siting, atmosphere – all these are important elements in achieving an appropriate contemplation of its meaning. This is what we refer to as the aesthetic and religious setting. It is conditioned by the structural materials (stone, lime, iron, wood), by the decorative materials (linen, wool, silk, flowers) and by the illumination (natural, such as oil or candles, or artificial, such as gas or electric lighting) and by anything else that might influence the dynamic of the image and the space created by all these factors.

Reading and understanding iconography

When preparing to contemplate an icon it is important to have made an adequate reading of the sacred page it represents. This will assist in understanding the aesthetic and symbolic elements of the iconographic theme in theoretical and practical terms.

When we wish to enter a state of prayer which flows from the Bible we start with a "reading" – a reading aimed, above all, at capturing the messages, suggestions and inspirations that arise from the sacred text and that present themselves to those who approach it with a religious attitude. To achieve something similar in the reading of icons, a suitable approach is also needed. The following stages are essential for this:

To "read" an icon like this one of the Presentation of Christ in the Temple, requires some knowledge of the sacred story it tells as well as other theological and patristic elements.

29

– Identification of the iconographic theme: what it represents.

– Elucidation of the theme, taking into account the biblical, patristic, liturgical, theological, aesthetic and technical antecedents and foundations it includes or that have inspired it.

– Interpretation of the figures, symbols, scenes and other iconographic elements of which it is composed.

– Special attention to the design, to the aesthetic structure of the composition and to the inverse perspective (from which the image must be contemplated) in order to identify, in an objective manner, the key areas of interest and to understand the semantic "maze" all this implies.[12]

– Recognition of the icon type that results from all this and that can be classified as one of the following: *panegyrist* (praise), *epic* (telling a story), *dramatic* (providing a contrast) and *dogmatic* (interpretative), according to the way in which the elements of the iconographic theme are treated.[13]

The greater our mastery of this whole process, the richer will be our reading of the icon.

Both the contemporary iconographer and the reader of icons must achieve the best possible understanding of the structure and the spirit on which the icon they are seeking to create or contemplate is based.

The point of departure is the same for both: a systematic reading of the original to identify the geometric structures that define its aesthetic composition.

This analysis or reading allows the contemplator or reader of icons to continue forward to aesthetic contemplation or religious prayer in which he will seek to synchronise with the creator of the work he is contemplating.

The iconographer, on the other hand, who seeks to copy this icon, undertakes the inverse of this process: bearing in mind the laws governing the geometrical structures of classic icons, he makes his design, using colour to bring it to life through his own contemplation and prayer.

Contemplation of an icon will reveal the geometric structures that determine its aesthetic composition.

The iconographer's reading is directed towards contemplation that will be transformed into the creation of his own icon, itself in turn a source of contemplation and prayer for himself and for others.

The reading made by an individual contemplating an icon ends in contemplation and prayer before the mystery presented by the iconographer.

The contemplative attitude

This is also the way to allow oneself to be absorbed by the image which, with this specific purpose, has the person who is praying as the centre of contemplation (inverse perspective). Placed thus we are in the best position to capture the global message of the icon and of the various iconographic elements and to allow ourselves to be immersed in the mystery before us. This is of great importance to understanding the original icon of Our Mother of Perpetual Help.

Similarly, as in the case of biblical texts, the better the preparation (remote and close, scientific and spiritual) of the person making the reading, the richer will be their understanding and their use of the icon selected. Symbols have a profound dimension that can only be understood with a particular religious sensibility. They speak and they are silent, they show and they conceal at one and the same time. The aesthetics of the icon demand a great effort of concentration and contemplation. And it is for precisely this reason that on entering the world of the sacred we spontaneously place ourselves in an environment of contemplative prayer.

This helps us to understand better why the eastern churches should have used icons as a means of evangelisation, of catechesis and theological study. In fact, as already mentioned, in the words of St John Damascene, "If someone asks you to demonstrate your faith to them, bring them to a church and place them before the sacred icons". The same remains true today, particularly in the case of those icons that offer us the great mysteries of the faith and of Christian life as their fundamental theme.

Historical context

To achieve the preparation described above it is essential to take account of the historical nature of icons, because not all are the same. On the contrary, if we study them carefully it is easy to discover a great diversity. Each period and each region has created its own examples with their own original message in response to very specific needs.

3. HISTORICAL DEVELOPMENT

The early Christians felt no need to use entirely new iconographic themes to express their faith in graphic form. They began by using the symbolic and aesthetic universe of the socio-cultural context in which they lived, particularly while the iconographic content of their compositions remained predominantly narrative.

Christians made use of the aesthetic forms of Roman art to express their faith, as can be seen in this Virgin Orante (Praying) with child, 4th century.

As time went by and as their artistic narrative began to acquire a more complex and original theological and aesthetic content, this became embodied in its own symbolic universe. The importance that art came to have in theological disputes in general, and in the iconoclastic controversy in particular, also contributed to this. It is therefore not surprising that a genuine "iconographic canon" should take shape against which the orthodoxy of images could be judged, in the same way as the orthodoxy of the written or spoken word could be judged against formulations of dogma. Yet even at that time it was not possible to dispense with the pre-Christian and local inheritance that has accompanied Christian art throughout its history.

Therefore, in order to understand the historical development of Marian iconography, we need to remember two fundamental elements: the development of theological thinking on the Mother of God and the general development of art in the Roman Empire. The former was responsible for the development of the themes and the latter for the changing forms adopted by these themes.

A) Theological thinking on the Mother of God

The development of theological thinking on the Mother of God was apparent in the Trinitarian and Christological disputes in particular and found official expression in the first seven ecumenical Councils. The last of these was specifically concerned with images and its influence began to be reflected in the

Byzantine mosaic giving expression in art to the doctrine of the first Councils on the Theotokos, the divine motherhood of Mary.

themes that Christian artists were asked to develop and in the emphasis of nuances within each work. Thus, for example, if we wish to understand the iconography of the *Pantocrator* and the *Theotokos* we must bear in mind the Trinitarian and Christological disputes that took place in the first ecumenical councils. The same is true of the iconoclastic controversies of 725 to 843 and the Second Ecumenical Council of Nicaea (787) with regard to the religious significance of icons in general (cf. Ch.11,2:1,4).

B) The general development of art in the Roman Empire: the key stages

If we limit ourselves specifically to icons and to the period from which Our Mother of Perpetual Help dates and the cultural area that produced this icon, we find five key stages in the development of art in the Roman Empire. We shall consider these briefly.

1. The Imperial Period (4th to 8th centuries)

The first period runs from the year 313 (the peace of Constantine) to 725 (the start of the iconoclastic controversy). The emperors Theodosius (392-408) and Justinian (527-565) were particularly influential and this was when the first icons appeared.

The relationship between these icons and the art of that period depends to a large extent on the position they were called upon to occupy at the period of the great imperial basilicas of Rome, Constantinople, Ravenna, etc. In these – whatever the setting – Christ almost always appears dressed in imperial purple and the Virgin Mary with the attributes of an empress.

The Virgin enthroned with the child and Saints,
6th century.

The first icons of the Pantocrator and the Hodegetria, which were to assume such importance in the later history of religious images, were created for the basilicas of this period. The spirit of imperial art and the doctrine of the great ecumenical councils referred to above are essential prerequisites to our understanding of these icons. The humble icon also becomes a reminder of and heir to the legacy of majesty that accompanies the sacred subjects it represents in the basilicas of that period.

At the end of this period, however, it was no longer merely a question of ritualistic images with a purely "decorative" purpose. Many of them, like relics before them, had become objects of veneration and expressions of theological ideas. It was this that gave rise to the iconoclastic controversies of 725 to 843.[14]

The Madonna of Comfort, 5th century. The face of the Hodegetria icon will be a key influence in later Marian iconography.

2. The Byzantine Style (9ᵗʰ to 11ᵗʰ centuries)

The second period begins with the "Triumph of Orthodoxy" (843) and ends with the Macedonian dynasty (867-1057). It is therefore known as the "Macedonian Renaissance" or the period of the Byzantine Renaissance. It culminates with the Emperor Basil II (907-1025).

It has been called the *golden age of the icon*. During this period artistic expression took on a greater realism, a more life-like relief and a more refined technique of the classical or Hellenic type. The content, on the other hand, emphasises the religious and transcendent meaning of the images, that had already made the icon something more than a mere aesthetic representation, transforming it into the bearer of a theological *presence*.

It was precisely "in this period, which produced the so-called 'Byzantine style' (between the 10ᵗʰ and 11ᵗʰ centuries in particular)" that the great diversity of eastern iconography began to emerge. "This was the result of a well conceived missionary effort by the Church which, during the 9ᵗʰ century, evangelised the Serbs and Bulgarians and a century later, the Russians, introducing its art together with its doctrine thanks to Greek artists who came from the metropolis or from the colonies on the Black Sea. The method used was essentially to translate the Byzantine rite into the language of the country and to create new 'communities' there that would imitate the 'Great Church' of Constantinople in every respect".[15] As a result, the lack of education in the faith among each of the populations being evangelised also produced a great diversity in the art of the icon, giving rise to national styles and schools even in their approach to the same iconographic theme.

Roman icon in the Byzantine style, 7ᵗʰ century, a synthesis of Hellenistic style and religious meaning.

Russian icon of the classical period, 12ᵗʰ century, displaying humanism, realism and harmony.

Russian icon of the desacrilization period, 15ᵗʰ century, showing greater expressiveness and emotional intensity.

3. The Classical Period (11th – 13th centuries)

The third period corresponds to the Comnenus dynasty (1057-1204). This was a period that produced "more ascetic ideals", particularly in the monasteries. Despite continuing with its earlier classical and humanist tendencies, art now achieved a "balanced, harmonious and perfect synthesis of classical realism and Christian spirituality". As a result, "the beginning of the 13th century can be considered as the "classical period" of the icon. This is also the period when the "Byzantine world" was definitively composed of the Balkan countries, Asia Minor, Georgia, Venice, southern Italy, northern Russia (from Kiev to Novgorod) and what was known as Suzdalia (Vladimir, Jaroslav, etc.)".[16]

4. The Period of Desacrilization (13th – 15th centuries)

The fourth period begins with the ending of the presence of the Roman Empire in Constantinople (1204-1261), with the Paleologus dynasty (1261-1453), which liberated the capital from the hands of the crusaders (1261), governed the destiny of the Empire up to the Turkish conquest of 1453 and produced a revival of the arts. From Constantinople, Byzantine culture spread to Georgia, Armenia, Serbia, Bulgaria and Russia (Suzdal, Novgorod and Pskov).

In iconographic art the lineal style of the 12th century was complemented by effects of light and shade that created a greater sensation of depth,[17] although each of the national schools brought its own interpretation to this. Thus, for example, M. Smirnova identifies three fundamental characteristics belonging to icons of this period from Moscow. Firstly, their expressiveness or emotional intensity – saints absorbed in silent, intense prayer, faces of the Virgin full of compassion and radiant kindness. Secondly, the lyrical and contemplative style, which accentuates the typical features of the Eleusa and which derives from this. The third characteristic he terms neo-classicism.[18]

Despite all this, religious art in general became increasingly secular, losing much of its transcendent spirit. More importance was placed on the image as an object than on the presence of the reality depicted. "If anything is projected in these works of art, it is the personality of the artist".[19]

Up to the middle of the 14th century, Constantinople continued to be the centre of Byzantine culture. After this time it gradually moved towards sites and schools on the periphery, such as Greece (Salonica, Cyprus, Crete and Mount Athos), Serbia, Bulgaria, Russia, etc, with aesthetic and thematic characteristics of which we should also be aware.

C) The Post-Byzantine School of Crete (1453-1669)

Historical background

The difficult political situation during the final stage of the Paleologus empire resulted in many artists emigrating to other Christian states and, in particular, to the island of Crete. A large number of refugees arrived on this island from the beginning of the 15th century. The fall of Constantinople in 1453 and that of Mistra in 1460 added still further to the number of artists coming to the island. This explains why, until its annexation by the Turks in 1669, Crete became the new centre of Byzantine art.

The Virgin of Mercy, 17th century. An example of the Virgin of the Passion from the Italo-Greek school. The angels were probably on the doors of the triptych.

The Paleologus Style or Second Renaissance we saw emerge during the final period of the Byzantine state found its greatest expression in the Cretan School and took the place of earlier styles. It was Cretan artists who, developing the Paleologus style, created the remarkable murals still preserved in certain churches and monasteries on Mount Athos, the monastic centre that managed to retain its independence despite the Turkish invasion. It was they who extended the splendour of the Third Golden Age of Byzantine painting into the 16th century. Between 1535 and 1568 they produced fifteen major murals on Mount Athos. Theophanes Strelitzas, the school's founder, decorated the churches of Lavra (1535), Stavronikita (1546) and Xenophontos (1563). His sons Neofitus and Simeon, his disciples Euphrosinos, Zorbis and Anthony and other unknown artists decorated the churches of Molyvoklissia (1536), Koutloumous (1540), Philcitheou (1540), Dionysiou (1542 and 1543) and Xenophontos (1544).

The Cretan School was clearly immersed in Byzantine art up to the 16th century. However, in the 17th century, the considerable contact that existed between Crete and Venice led to a rapid westernisation of the artists of the Cretan School. In fact, from the end of the 16th century many of them left the island for Venice where they trained in the art of painting. This explains the westernisation of Byzantine painting we are able to observe in many of the works that have survived.

When, at the end of the 16th century, the Cretan painter Michael Damaskinos painted the iconostasis of the Greek orthodox church of St George in Venice, his work still revealed its very close connection with the Byzantine tradition. However, it was here that the westernisation process of the Cretan School first began. Between 1571 and 1591 he also produced frescoes and a large number of icons that can now be found in the Monastery of Santa Catarina of Sinai, in that of Stavronikita (Mount Athos), in Zante, in Venice (Hellenic Institute collection) and in Candia (Church of St Menas).

Around 1600 the famous icon painter Andrea Rizo of Candia was working in Venice. He is considered to be possibly the author of the icon of Our Mother of Perpetual Help which is the subject of this book. His work continues to be closely linked to the Byzantine tradition, though there are details, such as the child's dangling sandal, that reveal his westernisation. Many of his works can be seen today in the Turin art gallery, the church of S. George in Venice and in the Florence gallery.

The icons produced by the most notable Cretan artists of the 17th century, such as Manuele Lambardos, Elias Moschos, Viktoros, Skouphos and Manuele Tzanes, show a rapid and progressive westernisation. This is revealed in the increasingly widespread use of elements typical of western painting such as the system of their work, the volumes, the classical perspective, the genuine luminosity, the taste for detail and the chiaroscuro.

The fall of Crete to the Turks in 1669 brought a large number of Cretan artists to Italy and the 18th-century post-Cretan Italian School completes the separation of the Byzantine tradition and its full immersion in western art. Only one Cretan artist managed to achieve universal fame by reconciling the Byzantine tradition with western art in a surprising and inspired way. This was Domenicus Theotokopoulos, 'El Greco' (1541-1614), whose originality among western artists can only be explained by taking into account his Cretan origins. As a result he was able, unlike any other western painter, to give his work that immense feeling of transcendence and spirituality that was so warmly embraced in Spanish religious circles of the Counter-Reformation.

The art of the icon in Crete

a) Candia, centre for the creation and diffusion of icons following the fall of Constantinople under Turkish dominion in 1453

Among the schools of iconography that flourished after the fall of the Byzantine Empire, that of the Island of Crete deserves a special mention. With its Cretan school (producing works that were balanced, settled, geometrically composed and also open to the influence of the Italian Renaissance) it eventually eclipsed all other Greek centres of iconography. In fact, although from an artistic point of view debate continues regarding the value and contribution made by this school, its importance is due to two specific factors: its relationship with Italian art and the position it came to occupy once Constantinople had fallen into the hands of the Turks.[20]

b) Venice embraces the icons of Crete

The Cretan School had originated in the 14th century under Master Pogomenos. However, its fame began to grow from the time the island became the principal territory of the Greek language and orthodox religion, free from the influence of Islam, being in the safe possession of the Venetians. Artists and scholars who had fled from Constantinople took refuge there, bringing with them their ancient traditions. The painter Theophanes the Greek, a native of Crete, also worked on the island before moving to Novgorod and was known as the Russian 'El Greco'.

"The group of painters who worked on the island during the 16th and 17th centuries was known as the Cretan School. At this period Crete became the most important centre of Greek painting. As a result of the Turkish occupation, icons were no longer produced in Constantinople or in the Balkan region, not even in Asia Minor . It is true that from the 16th to 19th century the traditional painting of mainland Greece continued to take its inspiration from the Cretan School, but it was frequently executed by peasants or uneducated monks."[21] The Cretan War (1645-1669) and the final fall of Candia into Turkish hands led to the forced emigration of many important painters who settled in the Ionian islands. At the same period, links with the Greek community in Venice were strengthened and it was to Venice that some of the most famous painters went.

The Virgin of the Passion with St John and St Nicholas by Andrea Rizo of Candia, 15th century, Basilica of St Nicholas, Bari.

c) General characteristics of Cretan painters

The Cretan School displays two main characteristics: one is that it reflects its eastern heritage; the other is its connection with western Italian art. The first explains its conservative nature, in keeping with the Paleologus tradition, which is also the source of its predilection for narrative themes, and for the Marian theme of the Hodegetria – this corresponds to the 13th to 14th centuries and to the first part of the 15th century. The second relates to the influence of Italian painting and can be seen, above all, in the choice of themes, in the humanisation of the figures and in the combination of colours.

The exhibition of Cretan icons held in Venice between 17 September and 30 October 1993 revealed a number of facts of great interest to the study of the Cretan school of iconography. For further study of this subject, cf. Nano Chatzidakis, D*a Candia a Venezia. Icone Greche in Italia XV-XVI Secolo.* "Venetiae quasi alterum Byzantium". (Catalogue of the exhibition held in the Correr Museum, Venice, 17 September to 30 October 1993. Fondazione per la Cultura Greca, Athens 1993, with Bibliogaphy.) It has the following to say on the characteristics of this school:

- classical and balanced compositions,
- flesh tones in shades of dark chestnut,
- small white highlights on 'sporgenti' (protruding) surfaces
- repetition of certain iconographic types throughout the 15th to 16th centuries: the Nativity, Christ's entrance into Jerusalem, the Resurrection, particular saints such as St John the Baptist, St Nicholas, St Anthony, St Demetrius, St George (on horseback or standing), St Phanuros and St Peter and St Paul.

41

This repetition can also be found in Italo-Cretan icons, where the most common themes are: the Madonna – of the Mother of Consolation type; Christ – of the Extreme Humility and Piety type; and among the saints the most common are St Jerome, St Francis and St Sebastian.

"Over the course of time the Creto-Venetian models were enriched by Renaissance types and poses, by realist architectural motifs and by spatial and landscaped backgrounds. In this way they became the vehicles of polished Renaissance compositions that would be used both in mural painting and in the icons of the Balkans ".[22]

"Many painters, influenced by Venetian taste, absorbed the useful elements this offered; others, however, moved gradually away from the Byzantine tradition to meet the demands of their rich Venetian clients and of Greek patrons with a taste for Venetian culture. There were also those who combined elements of the orthodox tradition with that of the Catholic, without concerning themselves with achieving genuine integration".

"During the 15th and 16th centuries, studios operated in some regions of Italy, principally Venice, Naples and Pola (Bari, Barletta) to satisfy the needs of Greek and Slav minorities who remained fiercely loyal to eastern worship and to the artistic traditions of the Middle Ages". "These studios maintained a close relationship with Cretan icon painters of the later period who shared the iconographic patterns of Byzantium but were also influenced by the Renaissance vision of man and beauty..."   Their work was disseminated "not only in Italy but also in the various regions of the Balkans, including the monasteries of Mount Athos. They therefore acquired great importance in the coastal region (the towns of Dubrovnik and Ragusa). In the 16th century some painters from these areas went to work in Italy and later returned to their native towns ."

The Cretan artists "developed a meticulous manner, characterised by great precision and by the use of bright light contrasting strongly with the faces, thus highlighting the forms". On the other hand, the "Greek artists working in Italy were replaced by a Greco-Italian school, based principally in Venice, that used darker colouring than the Cretan school and a lighter touch".

The original icon of Our Mother of Perpetual Help is an example of the Cretan School of the 14th to 15th centuries and belongs to the type designated *Virgin of the Passion* (cf. Chapter III, 3).

Notes to Chapter I

1 St John of Damascene: *De imaginibus*. Oratio I, PG, 94, 1247.

2 A. Grabar: *Le vie della creazione nell'iconografia cristiana: Antichità e medioevo*, Milan, 1988, 191.

3 P. Cortesi, F. di Palma, A. Vicini: *Icone Russe in Vaticano*. Bologna, 1989, 1.

4 E. Ros: *Reflexión sobre el icono sacro bizantino*. Barcelona, 1984, 32-33.

5 F. Ferrero: *Nuestra Señora del Perpetuo Socorro*, Madrid 1966, 254-256.

6 Grabar, 191-192.

7 Grabar, 192.

8 V. Lasareff and O. Demus: *Antiche icone russe*. Published by the New York Graphic Society in collaboration with UNESCO, 1958, 7.

9 cf. M. Massini: *Iniziazione alla "lectio divina": Teologia, metodo, spiritualità, prassi*. Padua, 1989, 2nd edition, 91.

10 Massini, 34-39.

11 In popular western religiosity we have a number of pious practices involving the use of icons as a means to prayer. For example, we have the *perpetual novena* to Our Mother of Perpetual Help, the *visiting* of Marian images and the *home visit* of the Most Holy Virgin. All these practices are, in essence, a time for contemplative prayer before an icon or image of Mary, the Mother of God. We can discover what this involves by referring to St Alphonsus de Liguori's book (1696-1787) on the *Visits to the Blessed Sacrament and to the Blessed Virgin Mary*, in which the saint invites us to adopt the same pattern of prayer before these two presences of the divine.

12 Babolin, *Icona e conoscenza*, Padua, 1990, 193-195.

13 cf. E. Sendler: L'icona, 66-73, which has examples of each type. Refer also to the illustrations listed below.

14 Ros, 14.

15 Ros, 14-15.

16 Ros, 15.

17 A. Massone, P. Manasse: *L'Icona – Arte e fede*, Rome, 1986, 28.

18 E. Smirnova: Moscow Icons 14th – 17th centuries. Leningrad-Oxford, 1989. Translated from Russian, 13-19.

19 Ros, 15.

20 cf. M.S. Calo, *La pittura del Cinquecento e del Seicento in Terra di Bari*, Bari, 1969, 14-72.

21 Massone-Manasse, 30-31.

22 cf. A. Bozhkov, Informe general sobre el peritaje de los iconos y demás valores artísticos e históricos en la Colección del Señor Rafael Onieva Ariza en "La Casa Grande", Torrejón de Ardoz, Madrid, Nov-Dec 1990, pro ms., 14-17.

The Basilica of Our Mother of Perpetual Help, Santiago, Chile.

THE ICONOGRAPHER'S PRAYER

T he painting of icons is a "divine art". It requires the exercise of asceticism to place oneself in the presence of God and in profound contemplation of the Sacred Mystery.

Before starting to paint, the iconographer recites the following prayer:

**You,
Divine Master of all that exists,
illuminate and direct
the soul, the heart and the mind
of your servant;
guide my hands
that I may represent
fittingly and with perfection
your image, that of your Holy Mother
and that of all the saints
for the glory,
joy,
and embellishment
of your Holy Church.**

CHAPTER II

THEMES OF MARIAN ICONOGRAPHY PREDATING THE VIRGIN OF THE PASSION

1. THE LEGACY OF A LONG PROCESS

2. FIVE FUNDAMENTAL THEMES AND MODELS:
   1) Mary, Virgin Mother of the Promised Messiah
      (2nd to 3rd centuries)
   2) Mary, Mother of God as Empress (4th century)
   3) Mary, Mother of God Praying (4th century)
   4) Mary, Mother of God Hodegetria (5th century)
   5) Mary, Mother of God Eleusa (11th to 12th centuries)

Notes to Chapter II

The Annunciation, 5ᵗʰ century mosaic celebrating the Theotokos, St Mary Major, Rome.

1. THE LEGACY OF A LONG PROCESS

The language of Marian iconography did not begin with the icons and certainly not with the icons of the Passion, of which Our Mother of Perpetual Help is one. The symbolic and artistic perfection of these works presupposes a long process of crystallisation of themes, patterns, techniques and aesthetic expression. They are the legacy of a long process of development.

Iconography, in fact, uses images in the same way as the written or spoken language uses words. When expressing ideas, structuring phrases or giving speeches, new words are not invented, rather those that already exist are used and combined in new ways.

Furthermore, this process is not random. All kinds of language involve a long history that is inherited and passed on spontaneously, but also in accordance with fixed laws of which the user becomes increasingly aware to the point where these are transformed into a "grammar". The language of iconography is no exception to this rule.[1]

Despite all this, "when one passes from one technical language to another, or from one generation of speakers to another, the terms that survive can change semantic form and value". However, full, absolute and authentic creativity is rare and the appearance of entirely new iconographic themes in the Christian world is virtually unknown after the period of their origination, though variants are certainly found.

According to Kondakov and Grabar, the origin of the most common representations of the Mother of God in the Middle Ages is to be found in the iconographic themes established in late Antiquity in order to narrate various scenes from the life of the *Theotokos*, the Mother of God. Thus, for example, the position of the figures in some icons of the Virgin in Majesty type can be explained by recalling the position they occupied when forming part of the *Adoration of the Magi*.[2] The same is true of other types of Marian icons and images in general, particularly where these show the Virgin caressing her son, feeding him at her breast or allowing herself to be caressed by him. The iconographic relationship between these themes and those of the *Virgin Mother* or the *Enthroned Sovereign* dating from late Antiquity, is quite obvious.

In fact, Marian iconography was, to some extent, inspired by the female portraiture (funerary or court) of the Greco-Roman world, by representations of the mother, particularly when dead (in the form of one praying, or of mother and child), by the "sacred images" of the emperors and empresses, and by the artistic forms that all these themes had gradually assumed in diptychs, seals, coins, monuments and the art of the period in general. In this way a number of themes and models of Marian iconography began to crystallise and gradually took on the form of icons themselves. Therefore, if we wish to understand the original and overall significance of such icons, we must refer back to the iconographic archetypes that produced them. And the same is true of specific icon types, such as the Virgin of the Passion, which we will be studying here. Here again we must go back to the archetypes and the iconographic legacy from which these icons derived or evolved. Such is our intention in this chapter.

The 3rd century portrait and 6th century mosaic of Empress Theodora constitute models of female beauty that would influence the depiction in icons of the face of the Mother of God.

2. FIVE FUNDAMENTAL THEMES AND MODELS

In doing this, however, we will disregard theories on the origin of the themes and models of Marian iconography and concentrate solely on their historical expression.[3] In this respect, and contrary to what the thematic diversity of Christian art might suggest, there is only a very limited number of archetypes from which such icons originally derive. Byzantine tradition attributes three to St Luke: the *Hodegetria*, the *Eleusa* and the *Orant (Praying)*. If to these we add other apparently independent Palaeo-Christian themes, we believe it is possible to identify five Marian archetypes that originally appear in a number of other fundamental iconographic themes or compositions: the *Virgin Mother*, the *Mother of God as Empress*, the *Orant*, the *Hodegetria* and the *Eleusa*. All other types and models, including the Virgin of the Passion, are derived from these five archetypes.

The first three (the *Virgin Mother*, the *Mother of God as Empress* and the *Orant – Sign and Deesis)*, considered as symbolic images in the Palaeo-Christian funerary cycle, form part of an iconography "that recalls and underlines the principal argument in favour of the salvation of all the faithful: the Incarnation of the Saviour and the Redemption he has brought to all people".[4] The presence of Mary as Mother in these iconographic themes or compositions is explained by the fact that this relationship with Christ is also what defines her relationship with God and with all people. Therefore, although all the types or models of Mary allude in some way to her divine motherhood, these three are the oldest and do so in a special way. Mary is the Mother of the Messiah promised by the prophets, the first person to recognise him as such (Lk 1:26-38 and 11:27-28) and also the first to present him in this way – to her cousin Elizabeth and to John the Baptist (Lk1:39-56), to the shepherds (Lk 2:1-19), to the aged

The Virgin Mother of the promised Messiah at the Epiphany with key elements, Mother and child, the prophet and the star. Inscription on a tomb in catacomb of Priscilla, Rome.

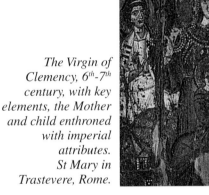

The Virgin of Clemency, 6th-7th century, with key elements, the Mother and child enthroned with imperial attributes. St Mary in Trastevere, Rome.

The Mother of God, "Great Panaghia", 11th-12th century, with key elements, the Mother of God Praying with the child in a medallion.

The Virgin of the Deesis, 15th century, Kremlin, Moscow, with key elements, the praying posture of the intercessor before Christ. the Pantocrator.

The Virgin of Prompt Help, 14th century, with key elements, with one hand the Virgin supports the child while drawing our attention to him with the other.

The Eleusa of the Passion with angels and saints, 18th century, Casa Grande icon collection, Madrid, with key elements, tenderness, the faces of the Mother and child touch as they lovingly embrace.

Simeon and to the prophetess Anna in the temple at Jerusalem (Lk 2:21-38), to the Wise Men (Mt 2:1-11) and to the guests at the wedding feast in Cana (Jn 2:1-11).

Moreover, when the Wise Men are searching for the "King" they find him in his mother's arms. It is therefore logical that artists should transform her into a "Queen and Lady", particularly at a time when monarchical figures had ceased to have any negative meaning for Christians.

The types or models of Mary offered by the *Hodegetria* and the *Eleusa* became fundamental iconographic types (archetypes) for Marian icons. Like the earlier models, on which they rely to some extent, these too depict the Mother of God, but accentuate certain characteristic elements.

The *Hodegetria*, for example, appears to accentuate her divine motherhood – in the icons she is the *Meter Theou*, the MP 0Y, the *Mother of God*. Christ is presented to us as the Logos with the gesture of speech or with the scroll of the Holy Word.

The *Eleusa*, on the other hand, focuses more on the human and maternal dimension of this Marian attribute. It underlines the humanity of the Son, whereas the *Hodegetria* places the emphasis on his divinity.

In both iconographic types, however, first the *face* of Jesus (with halo), then that of Mary, occupy the aesthetic centre of the composition. Special attention is also drawn to the *hands*. The hands recall the Virgin of the Incarnation, of the Epiphany, of the Deesis and of the Passion – these are hands that "support" Christ and "guide" us towards him, hands that intercede, the hands of a Mother holding the hands of her Son, the Word of the Father, the creative Word of God.

However, when interpreting these iconographic themes and, above all, when making use of them in prayer, we cannot lose sight of the relationship of Mary, the Mother of God, with the Church.

The iconostasis of orthodox churches where the icon of the Saviour is placed to the viewer's right and that of the Mother of God to the left.

In fact "even the iconostasis, which might be called the icon of the heavenly Church, has two centres in orthodox churches. To the right of the doors is the icon of the Saviour and, to the left, that of the Mother of God. The opening of these doors during liturgical celebrations symbolises the manifestation of the kingdom of heaven to all people, made possible through the Saviour and the Virgin Mary. Therefore, from the very dawn of patristic thought, the image of the Mother of God has been mystically identified with the image of the Church", and the relationship between the two "has been experienced through prayer".[5]

This is because of the place that Mary occupies in the mystery of salvation.[6] Hence, "the love and veneration for the Mother of God… that lie at the heart of orthodox piety and which form an organic and integral part of it". Mary's presence is therefore carried naturally and necessarily into all spheres of the Church's activities: liturgy, theology, architecture, art, literature, private piety. "It would be difficult to identify a single passage of the rich and varied orthodox liturgy, however small and particular it may be, that does not include an entreaty or prayer for help, intercession or gratitude to the Mother of God".[7]

It is therefore not surprising that something similar should occur with Marian icons. The Russian Orthodox Church has catalogued 601 of these that are considered as miraculous, and reproductions of them accompany the faithful everywhere.[8] So it is natural that if Jesus is considered as the icon of the invisible God, Mary should be considered the supreme icon of the Church. Mary is the expression of what the Church is called upon to be – "the 'Mary' of universal history".[9] The Marian experience of God thus constitutes a path to be followed by the whole Church and by each individual believer.

All icons of Mary are in some way icons of the Church and "the vocation of all Christians is, like Mary, to become living icons of the Church".[10] But more than this, we can see an iconographic formulation of many other key moments in the spiritual journey of Mary, of the Church and of each believer in the great themes of Marian iconography, through the relationship with the supreme mystery of the union with Christ, that is to say of the Church as the body of Christ and bride of the Lamb... But the mystery of the Church is also present in the fate of all souls", who can discover … "in the icons of the Mother of God, the fundamental stages of their spiritual life." "This very intimate relationship of the iconography of the Mother of God with spiritual life is the reason for its exceptional influence over the human soul."

The Mother of God as one Praying (Orant) is a symbol of the ascension of the soul, through the experience of death, towards the resurrection and participation in the mystical life of Christ. It culminates in the hereafter but we are also called upon to experience it at specific moments of our life on earth, such as times of prayer. This is why the celebrant raises his arms during the Eucharistic prayer and invites the faithful to raise their hearts to God, like Mary as the one Praying and in the scene of the Annunciation, the Ascension and Pentecost.

In the *Virgin of the Sign* and in the *Great Panaghia*, the praying theme is combined with that of the Mother of God. The *Virgin of the Sign* is worn by bishops in the form of a medallion on the chest and serves as a reminder that the mystery of the Incarnation must be experienced with a pure heart, like that of Mary, the Most Holy "Mother of God-made-Man". Through this "the mystery of the birth of Christ in the human heart is expressed not as a devotional metaphor but as a spiritual reality... By praying before such images a person is genuinely united with the divine archetype and, by being united with the mystery of the Incarnation, becomes ontologically a participant in this, experiencing it as a spiritual renaissance". This particular iconographic theme is especially popular in Russia.

In the blessing of the *Mother of God Hodegetria*, special reference is made to the words which, according to legend, were spoken by the Virgin to St Luke after he had painted her image: "Let the grace of he who was born of me, be with this image, through my intercession". If the *Virgin of the Sign* personifies the grandiose mystery of the incarnation and birth of Christ in the human soul, the *Hodegetria* represents the succeeding phase of the cosmic and personal development of this mystery. She is the guide, the one who leads the way along the path of Truth and Life. The image of the journey is one of the central images of the Bible. "When a living being departs from the path it leads to cosmic catastrophe."

Lastly, the icon of the *Mother of God Eleusa* is not the expression of an emotion or of a state of mind, which would obscure the spiritual vision, rather it is the elevation from image to Archetype. The Eleusa does not offer a moving depiction of the relationship between Mother and Son, instead it expresses the most profound experience of the life of the human soul in God, obtained not from a psychical perspective but in the world of the spirit."

The Mother of God, "Great Panaghia", by Jaroslav, 11th-12th century, Trejakov Gallery, Moscow, Kiev school. This icon represents the culmination of the theme of Mary Praying with her child, Emmanuel, in a disc or medallion (the Virgin of the Sign).

In this way "the soul is educated through the contemplation of the icons of the Mother of God. In the *Virgin of the Sign* the soul experiences in itself the mystery of the birth of Christ; in the icon of the *Mother of God Hodegetria* it finds the path it is called upon to follow; and in the *Eleusa* it experiences Christ as an internal reality."

We shall now consider each of the fundamental Marian types and themes to gain a better understanding of the Virgin of the Passion.

1) Mary, Virgin Mother of the Promised Messiah (2nd-3rd centuries)

This is the key theme. The Virgin holds the infant Jesus in her arms as a mother. She may be seated on a throne or simply standing. Sometimes she is shown embracing the child, feeding him at her breast or kissing him, while in other representations she appears in a more static pose.

The Mother and child, 3rd century fresco, Catacomb of Priscilla, Rome.

During the 2nd to 3rd centuries Mary appears seated. In some representations a prophet stands by her side with a scroll in his hand or gesturing to a star (the prophecy has been fulfilled). Other representations show scenes that recall the Annunciation (St Irenaeus tells us of the faith and obedience of Mary in this mystery), or are examples of what are known as "velata" (veiled), in which the Virgin of the Lord is shown seated, like a matron, but without the child. In the 4th century this iconographic theme was associated with that of "Maria orans", the Epiphany and the Birth of the Lord and gave rise to the iconographic themes of the Mother of God Orant (Praying) and the Virgin in Majesty, as we shall see below.

Sources of iconographic inspiration include the effigies of the beneficent empresses which appear on coins, and the images of dead mothers found on funerary monuments.

The oldest representation of this theme can be found in the scene of the *Virgin and child with the prophet Balaam* in the Arenario loculo in the catacomb of Priscilla in Rome.

"This is a fresco painting ... , in which Mary appears in a short-sleeved tunic, a veil covering her head, which is slightly inclined. She is seated on a chair without a back support and holds the naked child in her arms with maternal affection. In front of Mary stands the prophet Balaam – the prophet of light – dressed in a tunic and close-fitting pallium; with his right hand he gestures towards a star. This representation, of classical composition, is based on a passage in the Bible in the Book of Numbers 24:14-19 ..., although, according to some scholars, the scene could also have been inspired by passages from Isaiah 7:14 and 60:1-3 "[11]

The reason it is believed that this is the prophet Balaam rather than another prophet is because he is the prophet of the Gentiles and appears in the same posture in other catacomb paintings.

This representation is considered to be one of the oldest surviving paintings of Mary (dating from the early 3rd century).[12] The biblical texts to which scholars refer for interpretation are those indicated above. On the basis of these, iconographers have highlighted the following: the Emmanuel, the pregnant maiden, the dawn that illuminates the shadows, the glory of Yahweh, the kings who journey towards the brilliance of the awakening dawn, the mother of the Messiah.

The fact that this image is found in the catacomb of Priscilla suggests that its theological content is possibly related to the Marian theology of St Justinian, St Irenaeus and even that of St John the Evangelist. Moreover, its very presence in this area of burial gives it the soteriological character usually shared by the majority of 2nd and 3rd century representations in the Roman catacombs.

2) Mary, Mother of God and Empress (4th century).

In this theme Mary appears dressed as an empress, seated on a throne and either facing straight ahead or with her head slightly angled towards the child whom she holds in her lap, showing him to the figures in front of her or at her side.

The earliest examples of this theme, in the 3rd and 4th centuries, are associated with the *Adoration of the Magi*. In the Greek chapel of the catacomb of Priscilla, for example, "the Virgin is seated on a chair without a back support, holding the infant in her arms, while three figures, each of whom bears a gift in his hands, approach the Virgin and child".[13]

This subject became more strongly consolidated following the Council of Ephesus (431) and the Council of Chalcedon (451) at which Mary was proclaimed *Theotokos*. During the 5th century we find the grandiose mosaic cycle of the Liberian Basilica (triumphal arch), in which Mary

The Virgin of Clemency, 6th-7th century, St Mary in Trastevere, Rome. The Virgin in Majesty with imperial garments and throne – "As God himself became man within you, the greatest among the angels stand in awe before you who hold your infant in your lap."

appears as the Mother of God and Empress. There is also the Berlin diptych, the representation of Santa Maria Antiqua and the bas-relief of the door of the basilica of St Sabina in Rome. All these representations show us the Most Holy Virgin as Empress, Mother of God, Sedes Sapientiae and symbol of the Church.

From the 6th century onwards, the theme of the Virgin in Majesty begins to appear with a more pronounced imperial character in the great mosaic cycles of Constantinople, Ravenna, Parenzo, Salonica, Grado and many other basilicas in Rome.

During the 6th and 7th centuries it is already associated with the theme of the Egyptian and Armenian Hodegetria, which may well have derived from the early theme of the Virgin and child and reflect certain elements of the Christological and Marian theology of Alexandria.

During the 7th to 9th centuries greater emphasis was given to the regal aspect, with its accompanying decoration and the presence of holy figures. There are examples from this period in the underground Church of San Clemente, in the chapel of St Cenon, the basilica of St Praxedes, the apse of Santa Maria in Dominica, in Santa Maria in Trastevere with the Madonna della Clemenza, and in Santa Maria Antiqua.

This representation reached a new height in both East and West following the iconoclastic controversies. Later, Christian artists began to apply the imperial, regal or noble iconography of each period and region to their depiction of Mary. There are numerous variants.

The inspiration for the theme in which Mary appears as queen, revered by the angels and escorted by the apostles and saints, can be found primarily in the biblical account of the Epiphany (Mt 2:1-12), and later in the official iconographic patterns of the sovereigns (*sacrae imagines*), consuls and beneficent empresses. From here its influence crossed into themes such as the *Adoration of the Magi* (Mary enthroned with the infant), *Mary Praying* and *Mary with the infant in her arms*.[14]

For the Church, "the Epiphany is the manifestation of Jesus as Israel's Messiah, the Son of God and Saviour of the world". For the Gospel, the "Magi" coming from the East (Mt 2:1) and as "representatives of the pagan religions of neighbouring nations, signify the first of the nations to embrace, through the Incarnation, the Good News of Salvation". Their arrival "in Jerusalem to 'pay homage to the king of the Jews' " (Mt 2:2) demonstrates that, by the messianic light of the star of David (cf. Num 24:17; Rev 22:16), they seek in Israel he who will be king of all nations (cf. Num 24:17-19). Their coming means that the Gentiles cannot discover Jesus and adore him as the Son of God and Saviour of the world without approaching the Jews (cf. Jn 4:22) and receiving from them their messianic promise, as contained in the Old Testament (cf. Mt 2:4-6). "The Epiphany shows that 'the full number of the nations' now takes its 'place in the family of the patriarchs' (St Leo the Great, Serm. 3), and acquires the "Isrealitica dignitas" (is made 'worthy of the heritage of Israel').[15] There is also an allusion to this theme in the star that appears on the Virgin's forehead, although this relates to other iconographic themes not under discussion here.

3) Mary, Mother of God Praying (4th century).

There are two different representations in this type of Marian iconography. In one Mary appears without the child, her arms raised in an attitude of prayer, of entreaty and intercession, while she looks towards the faithful, inviting them to trust in her divine Son with whom she is interceding on their behalf.

The Virgin of the Deesis, 15th century, Kremlin Museum, Moscow.
The figure of Mary appears praying as intercessor before Christ, the Pantocrator.

In the other representation, Mary appears with the infant shown facing forward inside a medallion she wears on her chest – this is the Mother of God of the Sign, who carries on her breast the Emmanuel announced by Isaiah (pp 49 and 53). The Virgin also faces forwards, her arms raised in the posture of a person praying (orant). The biblical reference is as follows: "The Lord himself, therefore, will give you a sign. It is this: the maiden is with child and will soon give birth to a son whom she will call Emmanuel." (Is 7:14). The Gospel of St Matthew, quoted in the Advent liturgy states as follows: "Now all this took place to fulfil the words spoken by the Lord through the prophet: The virgin will conceive and give birth to a son and they will call him Emmanuel, a name which means 'God-is-with-us'." (Mt 1:22-23). It is specifically from these texts that the name of this iconographic theme is derived. It is a theme that culminates in the *Blacherniotissa* of Constantinople and the *Great Panaghia* to which the *Hagiosoritissa* and the *Peghe* also belong to some extent, although in the case of the latter (8th century), the Virgin may appear with the infant Jesus in her arms.

During the 6th to 7th centuries we find the image of Mary in iconographic themes such as the *Deesis*, the *Annunciation*, the *Visitation* and the *Ascension of the Lord*. Although the attitude of the Virgin is different in each of these – some focus on her intercession while others highlight testimony, praise or joy – all, however, add an imperial or regal quality to Mary's praying posture.

The image of the *orant* is very common in Palaeo-Christian cemeteries and sarcophagi and appears in the figure of a woman with her arms outstretched and slightly raised. At first this figure represented the *piety* (pietas) of the deceased person. Later it became an image of this, indicating that this was a pious person and began to acquire highly pronounced individual traits, like that of a *portrait*. In the 6th century saints and, in particular, martyrs began to be represented.[16]

In the Cimitero Maggiore in Rome, a 4th century painting shows a mother in prayer with the child in her arms and in a frontal position. "This could be Mary Orant and child. The other two figures of the arcosolium are making the same gesture as the mother. The Virgin's piety is expressed through the gesture of the ancient *pietas*, which is repeated in the Annunciation, when Mary bows to the will of God and accepts her mission to be the instrument of the Incarnation. Mary makes the same gesture in the scene of the Ascension. Like the angels who promise the apostles that Christ will return, in giving testimony to the second coming she repeats the gesture that indicated the first coming at the moment of the Annunciation." However, the image of Mary Orant in these scenes also recalls the Church and its mission here on earth.

Therefore, contemplating the iconographic type of Mary Orant in the context of the New Testament and the liturgy, which refer to the Mother of God, we are reminded, firstly of the *Virgin of the Annunciation and of the 'Fiat'*: "The Holy Spirit will come upon you, the angel answered, and the power of the Most High will cover you with its shadow." (Lk 1:35). "I am the handmaid of the Lord, said Mary, let what you have said be done to me." (Lk 1:38). The archangel Gabriel is therefore shown at her side and she is depicted as praying without the infant.

But we are also reminded of the *Virgin of the Visitation and of the Magnificat.* In response to Elizabeth's greeting Mary now adopts the attitude of prayer and the Mother of God, she raises towards him the great prayer of the Mother of the Messiah awaited and announced by the prophets: "And Mary said, My soul proclaims the greatness of the Lord..." (Lk 1:46).

It is from this double attitude that Mary is transformed into the "sign" of the promises made by God to his people and the symbol of the Church: she is the Virgin at Prayer, the intercessor, the mediatrix, Deesis.

4) Mary, Mother of God Hodegetria (5th century).

The Hodegetria is the most complete representation of the Mother of God. "In this Mary appears in a frontal position, her eyes fixed on the viewer. She is usually depicted in half-figure, but is also shown full-length, seated or standing. Carrying the child on her left arm, she wears a green tunic and red mantle (maphorion) and her hair is completely concealed inside a kind of cap that she wears under the attached veil."

"The child, also in a frontal position, though turning slightly towards his mother, is seated on her left arm. With his right hand slightly raised he gives a blessing in the Greek style, while in the left he holds a parchment scroll, the symbol of prudence and wisdom and the traditional attribute of the prophets. He is both child and adult, the Emmanuel, and has the attributes of divinity: a cruciform halo with the inscription O Ω N [he who is], and the monograms IC XC [Jesus Christ] at the sides. The monograms of the Mother, located on each side of her head, are MP 0Y [Meter Theou: Mother of God].[17]

The "canonical" or officially recognised types of the Hodegetria display a solemn majesty, and a sacred and somewhat static quality.

The Hodegetria of Tichwin, 18th century, Redemptorist archive, Rome.

Origin and meaning

To understand this iconographic theme it is important to be aware of a number of events that took place in the early 5th century. They are the following:

– the growing importance of the portrait in Christian iconography;

– the impetus given to veneration and to the official images of the Virgin Mary by the Councils of Ephesus (431) and Chalcedon (451);

– the construction of Marian basilicas in Constantinople and Rome: the basilica of S. Maria Maggiore was completed around 440;

– the importance of the relics found in Palestine, which include the portraits of Mary attributed to St Luke.

Etymologically, the title of Hodegetria means "the guide who shows the way". When applied to the image of Mary venerated in Constantinople it can refer to:

– the iconographic composition in which Mary, with her right hand, gestures towards Christ who is the believer's true way;

– the name of the shrine in which the image was displayed and which had begun to be known by this name because army chiefs (guides) used to meet there to ask for divine protection before going off to war;

– the pious legend according to which the Virgin appeared to two blind people and guided them to this shrine where they recovered their sight.

The first Hodegetria

Whatever name it was known by, one thing is certain, in the year 438 a large copy of an image venerated in Palestine as a portrait of the Virgin was made and brought to Constantinople where it became known as the Hodegetria. This image of the Virgin was reproduced by a Byzantine artist and was sent in turn to Rome in the autumn of 439.

This explains why the "oldest Marian icon" of which we are currently aware is preserved in the sacristy of the church of S. Francisca Romana. This shows the heads of the Virgin and child painted on linen cloth using the encaustic process. Its dimensions are impressive. The face of the Virgin is 33.6 cm wide, "while the head measures 54 cm from the upper part of the forehead to the edge of the tunic. This is two and a half times larger than life. Taking the rest of the image in proportion, and bearing in mind that the Virgin was certainly depicted on a throne, the image is some 3.40 m high and 1.10 m across."[18]

M. Guarducci believes this Roman image to be a direct and faithful copy, almost contemporary with the original Hodegetria, made on cloth using the 'impronta'[19] technique and taken from the panel of the archetype, as happened with relics. As a result, in this image the 'left' becomes the 'right' and vice versa. This explains the unusual and abnormal representation of the infant on his Mother's right arm, while she gestures towards him with her left.[20] In fact this is a *Dexiocratousa* Hodegetria (in which the infant is carried on the right arm) whereas such images are more commonly A*ristocratousa*, i.e. the infant is supported on the left arm, while the Virgin gestures towards him with her right.

This first Hodegetria is one of the seven Marian icons of Rome attributed to St Luke. All scholars agree that this formed part of the oldest known Marian icon. The technique and the iconography of the faces recall "the ancient art of tomb portraits from the Egyptian world and culture", particularly that of Alexandria.[21] Some scholars, however, do not consider this image to be a "copy" but an original Marian iconographic type, predating the Byzantine Hodegetria itself. All the details of this image described above have their own meaning. Although discussion of such matters does not form part of our purpose here, it seems certain that this is indeed "as far as one is aware, the oldest official image of veneration of the Virgin in East or West". The image is known as the *Madonna of Comfort*.

The Madonna of Comfort, 5ᵗʰ century, Basilica of St Francesca in the Forum, Rome.

The face of the Theotokos

It would also seem that this "face of Mary, which has come down to us miraculously intact and fresh, reveals some traits that Epifanio, Jorge Cedreno and Nicéforo Calisto attribute to the Virgin when describing her physical appearance. These traits are in fact common characteristics of feminine beauty as dictated by the literary canons of the period".[22]

Whatever the case, discussions of the icon of *Santa Maria Antiqua* appear to confirm the existence of a Marian iconographic type that corresponds to that of the Hodegetria and with three specific historical examples: the "St Luke image" venerated in Palestine, the Hodegetria of Constantinople and the copy preserved in Rome. Therefore, taking into account the possible variants of the original archetype and its *impronta,* it is not difficult to explain the origin of the icons of this type known to us thus far. From the 11th century onwards a countless number of these were produced. Those of the earlier period, however, are much rarer. Among these is the icon preserved in the Pantheon in Rome (7th century).

Salus Populi Romani, 12th century, a Hodegetria, St Mary Major, Rome.

The main differences identifiable in the various types relate to the figure of the child. For this reason the theological significance of the Hodegetria becomes clearer if we bear in mind how it differs from the other iconographic type – the *Eleusa* – that we will now consider.

5) Mary, Mother of God, Eleusa (11ᵗʰ to 13ᵗʰ centuries).

The *Eleusa* (merciful, kind, compassionate) differs from the *Hodegetria* (she who shows the way) in the posture of the child. The Virgin carries him in her arms (usually supporting him on her right arm, although she may also use the left), clasping him to her and, inclining her head, brings her face close to that of her Son.

"The *Eleusa* abandons the static quality of the *Hodegetria* ... and displays a clear and undeniable feeling of affection and tenderness. The face of the Mother and child are brought close together, the two figures exchange caresses and the child's affection is even shown in the way in which he places his arm around his Mother's neck. The term *Eleusa* refers specifically to the loving attitude of the Mother which arouses the pity (*eleos*) and compassion of her Son for the faithful and also to the mutual affection between Mother and her Son".[23]

The Virgin of Vladimir, 11ᵗʰ-12ᵗʰ century, is the prototype Eleusa, displaying a strong feeling of affection and tenderness, abandoning the strict Hodegetria model.

Origin and meaning: the radiance of divine love

The iconographic theme of the Eleusa appears to have originated in the Byzantine world after the iconoclastic controversies (of the 8th to 9th centuries) and prior to the 12th century, some actual examples of this period having survived. After that it began to spread to the West and into Russia. It is therefore not the result of the influence of western art.[24]

But although this iconographic theme did not begin to spread until that time, it is possible to find its antecedents in the same profane sources that inspired the artists of the earlier theme. We can also assume that, like other Marian iconographic themes, it existed as early as the 6th and 7th centuries although conditions did not lend themselves to its diffusion until the period indicated.

The most famous example of this type is the image known as the *Virgin of Vladimir* (which dates from the end of the 11th century or early 12th century). But the theme also appears in other iconographic representations of the same period. In these the Virgin is sometimes shown as a half-figure, sometimes full-length and standing, but there are also examples in which she is shown seated. The last two types are the predominant ones in western art.

The Virgin's posture recalls the Hodegetria, the original of which shows her full-length. However, the close proximity of the head of the Virgin with that of the child, together with the child's movements, turn this into a new iconographic type "expressing the intimacy between the Mother of God and her divine Son". This is how he appears in some icons and in western art: "the child appears in a natural manner, playing in the arms of his Mother who appears full of joy and happiness".

Our Lady of Grace, 16th century, Redemptorist archive, Rome.

Despite all this, "the icon of the Mother, her head inclined tenderly towards her Son, and the representation of the child, who embraces his Mother, is not the expression of God made man but of the radiance of divine love. The solemn demeanour is transformed into a vision of intimacy, an intimacy in which human nature, with all its richness, is penetrated by the divine light. The icon of the Eleusa therefore expresses a completely different concept from that of the Hodegetria".

The shadow of sorrow and intimation of the Passion

But there is something more. "*The Virgin of Tenderness* and, in particular, the *Virgin of Vladimir* and variants thereof, reveal another aspect we should note. The intimacy between Mother and Son is often mixed with sadness. Let us recall that the close proximity of the faces of Jesus and Mary is a gesture that appears in the 11th century in two scenes related to the Passion of Christ. In the scene of the *Presentation*, it is Simeon who, with prophetic words, evokes the suffering of the child and the suffering of the Mother. The other scene, commonly known as the *Compianto*, also forms part of the Passion. This is where Simeon's prophecy is realised. The Mother holds in her arms her Son who has been taken down from the cross. Her face is marked by immense pain – the pain of a mother grieving for her dead son, but also the pain of one who knows the mystery of evil and the suffering of all people." (p.68)

"According to Andrej Rublev, the meaning of the Passion is confirmed by a representation found on the reverse side of the Vladimir icon: it shows a symbolic representation of the death of Christ on the cross."

All of which leads us to conclude that, from the 11th century onwards, the theme of the Eleusa began to be associated in a special way with the theme of the Passion and of forgiveness. The church in Constantinople where the Eleusa was venerated was known in Latin as "Sancta Maria Misericordiae". "Mary, united with her Son in the sacrifice of his life to atone for the sins of the world, intercedes with him on behalf of all those who seek her help. Therefore, the various names, although important in terms of the classification of iconographic types, reflect a single reality – that of the love of God, with Mary as the favoured instrument."[25] The Virgin of Vladimir is the finest example of this concept.

It has also been said that "emphasis should not be placed on the Virgin's tenderness as a mother towards her child, but on how she moves her Son to intercede on people's behalf. The Slavic term *Umilenie*, used to translate the Greek term *Eleusa,* is an expression of this. In fact, in the term '*Spasovo umilenie*' it is the infant Jesus who seeks the protection of his Mother from the sufferings of the Passion and the sorrows that await him. The Greek word *Eleusa*, with its notion of mercy and compassion has nothing in common with the Slavic term *Umilinie*, which soon appears in Russian medieval records with the sense of caress."[26]

Tenderness and sorrow: an iconographic reading of the Eleusa

"In the iconography of Byzantine art, the head of the Virgin and that of her divine Son are placed symbolically close together. This gesture expresses the fact that Mary is always close to God. It is a vision of the Theotokos, the source of divine grace, that resides in her through the Incarnation of the Logos and of her own grace that pours forth through her compassion."

"... In the *Eleusa*, the Mother does not embrace her Son with joy and happiness, filled with affection, nor does the infant Jesus play with his Mother in the innocence of childhood. What they express is terror, faced with the impending vision of the suffering that awaits him on the cross and through which he will redeem all people. The Mother of the Saviour, for her part, a symbol of divine mercy and mediatrix of the whole human race, is not depicted taking pleasure in the presence of her Son, as claimed in apocryphal

The Virgin of Panumnitos, a Bulgarian icon, 16th-17th century. One of the most famous examples of the "Tenderness" model. The Virgin's face betrays a hint of sadness, while the child clings to his Mother as if seeking protection from the suffering of the Passion that awaits him.

accounts and most interpretations by Byzantine scholars who have studied the Eleusa icon type ... The Virgin Theotokos suffers the sorrow that awaits her Son. Her face always shows concern rather than joy. She is at once the compassion of the world, the mercy of the divine will and mother of mercy..."

"In short, the name *Eleusa* does not apply to only one iconographic type. Rather it is a dogmatic definition formulated with great success by the poets of Byzantium. It is a concept to identify the Logos made flesh and turned over to the Passion and the divine Mother in her function as mediatrix for the Redemption of the world."[27]

"Thus, the drama of the Logos incarnate and the sufferings of the Mother of God were able to find expression in the single word *Eleusa* in the Byzantine world, while artists invented a number of variants to give form to the dogmas of the Passion and the Redemption." The variants of the *Eleusa*, so closely associated with the concept of the Passion, are therefore no more than a reflection of a development that led gradually to the Rizo of Candia model. In this, the angels hold in their hands the instruments of the Passion and the image includes an explanatory verse.

Principal Variants

A classification of the Marian types designated as *Eleusa* will include the following:

- The *Virgin of Vladimir*, in which the Virgin Mother of God has the Christ Child on her right arm and gestures towards him with her left; the infant Jesus brings his face close to that of his Mother and embraces her, as if seeking refuge and shows the sole of his left foot (cf. p.64).

- The *Glykophiloussa* (Virgin of the sweet kiss) who not only cherishes the child affectionately (supporting him either on her right or left arm), but also shows Mother and child embracing tenderly, with the child placing his arms around his Mother's neck (cf. pp.65 and 67).

- The *Pelagonitissa*, which reveals the greatest degree of emotion of all the preceding iconographic variants (cf. p.70).

- The *Kykkotissa* in which the Virgin Mother of God holds Christ. The child turns his head away, full of consternation; in his hand he holds a scroll which, if inscribed, usually quotes the words of Lk 4:18, though occasionally those of Is. 62:1 (cf. p.70).

- The *Virgin of the Passion*, which has a number of variants. The Russian version is known as the *Strastnaia*, derived from the liturgical term "Strastnoi" which refers to the Passion of Christ[28] (cf. Ch. III, p.89).

The iconographic theme of the *Eleusa* therefore leads spontaneously and specifically to the theme of the Virgin of the Passion, to which the icon of Our Mother of Perpetual Help belongs.

The Bridegroom, 19th century Russian icon demonstrating the relationship between the theme of tenderness (Eleusa) and that of the Passion.

Eleusa of the Passion, 16ᵗʰ century, Redemptorist archive, Rome. Note the closeness of the faces, the clasping of hands, and sole of the foot losing its sandle.

Left – The Russian Eleusa Kikkotissa, 17th century. The icon takes its name from Mount Kikkos (Cyprus). The adolescent child displays his bare feet and holds in his hand a scroll with text.

Right – Drawing of the Pelagonitissa. Note the strong accentuation of the emotional aspects.

Notes to Chapter II

[1] cf. A. Grabar: *Le vie della creazione nell'iconografia cristiana: Antichità e medioevo*. Milan, 1988, 51.

[2] cf. Grabar, 196.

[3] In this section we shall be repeatedly using a number of terms the meaning of which we would like to clarify at the outset. Thus, the term *composition* is used in the normal sense that applies when dealing with works of art: a piece of iconography as a whole with its own meaning. Closely related to this is the *pattern* or fundamental and characteristic structure of the composition. We refer to this as the *theme* when it expresses an idea or represents something that gives conceptual unity to the piece of iconography as a whole. Likewise, we talk of an iconographic *type* or *model* to refer to a figure that displays a number of characteristic iconographic features and elements that distinguish it from others. Both terms include the idea of something characteristic or exemplary from which certain characteristics of other figures may be derived. It is for precisely this reason that we use the term *archetype* to refer to the original type or model, not derived from any other iconographic model in terms of its archetypal quality, although this may certainly be projected on to other icons.

[4] cf. Grabor, 29

[5] V. Ivanov: *L'iconografia della Madre di Dio*, in Various Authors., *La Madonna a Mosca e a Roma. Teologia, arte, devozione popolare*, Edizioni Paoline – Patriarcato di Mosca, Cinisello Balsamo (Milan), 1992, 29.

[6] V. Nikitin: *La Madre di Dio nella letteratura russa*, in Various Authors, *La Madonna a Mosca e a Roma,* 109.

[7] Metropolita Sergij: *La Madre di Dio nella Chiesa ortodosa*, in AA. VV., *La Madonna a Mosca e a Roma*, 152.

[8] L. Lebedev: *Il culto delle icone mariane*, in Various Authors., *La Madonna a Mosca e a Roma*, 68.

[9] B. Forte: *Maria nella teologica occidentale. Breve sintesi di teologia mariana*, in Various Authors., *La Madonna a Mosca e a Roma*, 152.

[10] V. Ivanov, op. cit. 29f. The quotations which follow in this section are from Ivanov.

[11] S. Carletti: *Catacumba de Priscila*. Rome, 1985, 23-24.

[12] Carletti, 24, cit. 8. *The Catechism of the Catholic Church*, London, 1994, states the same on the back of the fragment of the fresco reproduced in *The Catechism* facing page 13.

[13] Carletti, 31.

[14] Grabar, 105, 108 and 197.

[15] *The Catechism of the Catholic Church*, London, 1994, n. 528; cf. also nos. 122, 439, 555, 711-716, 1171, 2177.

[16] cf. Grabar, 102-103.

[17] G. Gharib: *Le icone mariane: storia e culto*. Rome, 1987, 88.

[18] M. Guarducci: *La piú antica icone di Maria: un prodigioso vincolo fra Oriente e Occidente*. Rome 1989, 32.

[19] An "impronta" is the image that is produced by the application of another image on to appropriate materials. This is the process used in seals which are prepared using the 'negative' of the image required, to give the 'positive' of the image when produced. However, in the case of ordinary images, *impronta* produces a negative. This is the same as happens with the 'reflection' of an image viewed in a mirror, i.e., the mirror image.

[20] Guarducci, 82.

[21] P. Amato (ed.): *Imago Mariae*. Tesori d'arte della civiltà cristiana: Roma, Palazzo Venezia, 20 giugno – 2 ottobre 1988. Rome, 1988, 22-23.

[22] Guarducci, 82

[23] Gharib, 91.

[24] cf. E. Sendler: *La Vergine della Tenerezza*. Pro ms. taken from "Plamia", 71 (1987), 3-23, by the "Russia Ecumenica" centre, Rome, 2. cf. Sendler, 3-9 throughout this section.

[25] Sendler, 9.

[26] M. Tatic-Djuric: *Iconographie de la Vierge de Passion. Genèse du dogme et des symboles*, in "De cultu mariano saeculis XII-XV" Acta Congressus mariologici mariani internationalis Romae anno 1975 celebrati. Vol. VI. *De cultu mariano in litterarum studiis et in arte religiosa*, Rome 1981, 135-169, with 21 graphic docs., 138.

[27] cf. M.Tatic-Djuric, 139-140, for this section.

[28] cf. F. Ferrero: *Nuestra Señora del Perpetuo Socorro. Proceso histórico de una devoción mariana.* Madrid, 1966, 112; C. Henze: *Mater de Perpetuo Succursu. Prodigiosae Iconis Marialis ita nuncupatae monographia*, Bonn am Rhein, 1926, 20-21.

The Church of Our Mother of Perpetual Help, Madrid, Spain.

CHAPTER III

THE VIRGIN OF THE PASSION

1. ANTECEDENTS AND SIGNIFICANT EXAMPLES

2. CHARACTERISTICS AND VARIANTS

3. THE CRETO-VENETIAN SCHOOL

Notes to Chapter III

T he iconographic compositions known as *Virgin of the Passion* share the following fundamental characteristics.

– The presence of the instruments of Christ's Passion in the scene of the Virgin and child, usually carried by angels or archangels and sometimes accompanied by Latin or Greek inscriptions.

– The movement of the infant Jesus, who looks in the direction of these instruments or towards a point external to the composition itself and who, in alarm, seeks refuge in the hands or arms of his Mother, the sole of one of his feet being exposed, his sandal having fallen from his foot in the sudden movement and now dangling by its laces.

– The attitude of the Virgin who gazes into the distance as if contemplating the suffering of her divine Son while she holds him tenderly.

The Virgin of the Passion, 15th century, by Andrea Rizo of Candia, Basilica of St Nicholas, Bari.

1. ANTECEDENTS AND SIGNIFICANT EXAMPLES

At first sight, the Virgin of the Passion appears to be an iconographic representation of the portent of the Passion for Christ and for his Mother.[1] The biblical source of the theme can be found in the Presentation of Jesus in the temple (Lk 2:22-39). In the iconographic representation of this scene, Byzantine and Russian art accentuates the attitudes of the principal figures: Mary's offering, the hope and reverence of the aged Simeon on holding the infant in his arms and the prophetess Anna's gesture towards the Saviour (cf.p.29).

As discussed in the previous chapter, some authors also consider this "portent of the Passion" to be a standard element of the iconographic theme of the Eleusa, which therefore requires an explicit reference to the idea of the Passion always to be present in the attitudes of Jesus and Mary.

But that is not all. "The portent of the Passion had already been expressed by Romanus Melodos (c. 560 +) in the second hymn of the Nativity", relating it, naturally, "to the prophecy of the aged Simeon (Lk 2:35), who on the day of the Presentation of Jesus in the temple told the Virgin that a sword of sorrow would pierce her heart. Hence the eastern representation of the *Virgin of the Passion.*"[2]

However, the theme as presented by Romanus Melodos includes a dialogue between Jesus and Mary, which also involves Adam and Eve. In fact, according to this, Adam and Eve are going to the grotto. They are met by the Virgin who presents their requests to the infant Jesus. The following conversation takes place between Mother and Son:

Jesus: "I am overwhelmed by the love I feel for humankind. My Servant and Mother, I do not wish to sadden you. But I will tell you what I am to do and will respect your soul. One day you will see the child you carry now in your arms with his hands pierced by nails out of his love for your kind. He whom you feed, others will feed him bile; He whom you call life, you will have to see hanging on the cross and you will mourn his death. All this will I bear gladly out of the love I have always felt and continue to feel for all people, the love of a God who wants nothing but to be able to bring salvation".

Mary says: "Oh root of my life, let not the ungodly harm you! My son, let me not see you immolated when you are grown into a man!"

Jesus replies: "Weep not, Mother, over that of which you know nothing: if these things do not come to pass all those for whom you plead will perish. Oh Mother, full of grace, consider my death but a dream. After three days in the tomb I shall rise again and bring new life to the earth and to all who dwell there. Mother, go forth and tell these things and be joyful in them."

Mary says to Adam and Eve: "Be patient still. You who acclaim me 'full of grace' have heard what he is willing to suffer on your behalf."[3]

P. Milijkovik-Pepek, "by stressing the coincidental nature of the iconography of the Presentation in the Temple with that of the Virgin of the Passion, which shows the same distraught gesture of the infant who turns away his head, full of tragic foreboding, has found an explanation for this with a theological foundation."[4]

According to M. Cattapan the oldest icon with the theme of the Passion is that of Our Mother of Perpetual Help in the Church of Sant' Alfonso in Rome.[5] He believes that it dates back to between 960 and 1000 (early 11th century). However, although we know of some representations of the Virgin and child which include references to the Passion and date back to the 12th century,[6] the style of the icon and the presence of the archangels St Michael and St Gabriel with the instruments of the Passion would seem to indicate a much later date. We must therefore seek out other origins and antecedents for the Rome model.

Elsewhere we have mentioned the mural belonging to the church of Santa María de Tahúll (in Lérida, Spain) and preserved in the Museum of Catalonian Art in Barcelona, room VI, no. 15.961. This shows an angel presenting a Latin cross to the infant Jesus and is a portrayal of the Virgin in Majesty. It dates from the 12th century.[7]

However, the image considered to be the oldest representation of the Virgin of the Passion and including the instruments of Calvary carried by angels, dates from the end of the 12th century and appears in a fresco in Arakos (Cyprus, 1192). In this, the Virgin is standing with the infant Jesus asleep on her right arm while two angels above show the instruments of the Passion. The Virgin of the Passion in the monastery of Zica is similar, though in this image Mary carries the child on her left arm and the archangel with the instruments of the Passion is on another wall. This fresco probably dates from the years 1207-1220.

There are also other 13th-century representations in which the theme of the Passion appears to be explicitly related to that of the Glykophiloussa which, in itself "is not a single theme, but an iconographic type considered and treated as a Virgin of the Passion". An example of this is the Mount Sinai icon of the Passion.

In the 14th century we find an example from Macedonia in which the instruments of the Passion are carried by a single angel. There is also the icon of San Fantino from Venice, which dates from the second half of the 14th century or the early 15th century at the latest.[8]

The Virgin of the Passion theme dates from 12th century. One of the earliest is this 13th century "Virgin of Sinai".

The writings of St Brigid of Sweden (1302-1373), a Third Order Franciscan, include accounts of visions in which the Virgin spoke to her of her prior contemplation of the Passion and of her sorrow at the Passion and Death of Christ. The *Revelations* of this saint have been related to iconographic theme of the Virgin weaving "the tunic of Christ" alongside the infant who gestures towards the angels carrying the cross.[9] During the 14th century the theme of the Passion is also found in Serbia, becoming most widespread during the 15th and 16th centuries through the efforts of the Cretan iconographers, as we shall see below. Later it is found in another icon type. However, the theme we are studying here must not be confused with those in which the instruments of the Passion appear and are associated with the Final Judgement or with the image of Christ in glory.

"But, in my opinion, iconographically speaking, the definitive forms of the Virgin of the Passion, with its complete repertory (of characteristic symbols) comes directly from the Kykkotissa and from the Virgins of the Consolation, to which only the angels with the instruments of Calvary have been added. On the island of

Cyprus we find examples of Glykophiloussas in this characteristic attitude, which would later become common to post-Byzantine iconography." [10]

2. CHARACTERISTICS AND VARIANTS

The characteristics and variants found in the icons of the Virgin of the Passion are associated primarily with the iconographic type of the Virgin, the child and the Angels. There is also the title, the abbreviations that accompany the various figures and the literary texts that form part of the composition. To all of which can be added the characteristics of the various authors and schools in respect of each of the elements mentioned.

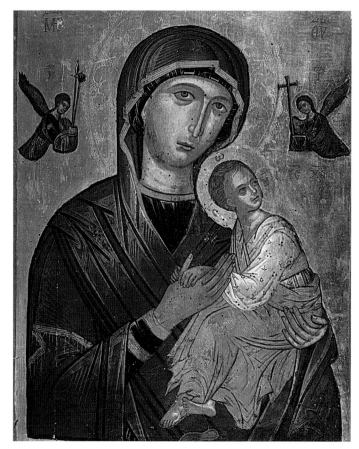

The Virgin of the Passion, 17th century, Redemptorist archive, Rome.

However, the dynamics of the process that leads to the iconographic theme of the Virgin of the Passion, and that culminates with the Cretan school appears to be marked by the appearance of the following iconographic elements:

– the movement of the foot of the infant Jesus, showing the sole of the foot in a variety of different ways.

– the placing of the hand of Christ in Mary's "Hodegetria hand", while with the other hand he holds the scroll or makes a gesture of speech.

– the proximity of the faces of the Virgin and child. It is specifically this that has led some scholars to compare this posture with that in compositions of the "Compianto di Cristo". In this context it is interesting to point out another reason for associating the theme of the "Compianto" with that of the Virgin of the Passion: the "Compianto di Cristo" attributed to Teodoro Poulakis (1622-1692) (cf. M. C. Bandera Viani, n. 44, pp 36-37), shows two winged angels with the instruments of the Passion that also appear in the scene of the Descent of Jesus into Limbo and which seem to recall the scene described by Romanus Melodos.

– the infant Jesus embracing the Virgin.

– the presentation of the instruments of the Passion in the hands of the angels in Marian icons with a variety of iconographic themes relating to the Mother of God.

– the movement of the infant's head, which appears to be looking towards these instruments or to a point outside the composition itself.

In the Creto-Venetian school, the instruments of the Passion appear to be the same as found in certain icons of the *Anastasis, Resurrection or Descent of Christ into Limbo* and which represent the Resurrection of Christ. This is one of the most significant contributions made by the school to the iconographic theme of the Virgin of the Passion. It could even be said to be the starting point for the different models which began to appear later, including those of the Russian schools.

Th Virgin of the Passion by Emanuele Lambardos, 16ᵗʰ-17ᵗʰ century, Bazantine Museum in Athens, Creto-Venetian school. Eleusa type with clear indications of the Passion.

If this is the case, the instruments of the Passion, in the specific theme under study here, represent an explicit reference to the glorious Passion of Christ.

In the West, however, the portent of the Passion, alludes to the symbolism of the sword that will pierce the heart of the Mother of God as referred to in Simeon's prophecy. This symbolism is also made explicit in the instruments of the Passion. Moreover, just as in eastern iconography of the *Anastasis*, it is Christ who enchains and destroys the power of the devil, here it is Mary who does so with the instruments of the Passion. In these representations we can see an allusion to the *Virgin of Help*: Mary brandishes a club, mace or stick to free the child over whom the devil seeks to gain control.

The Virgin iconographic type

The iconographic type of the Virgin varies greatly in icons of the Passion. Before arriving at the definitive type created by Rizo, derived from the Hodegetria and very similar to that of the icon of Our Mother of Perpetual Help, it adopted fundamental iconographic elements from all the different Byzantine Eleusa types. As M. Tatic-Djuric comments, "The Virgin of the Passion, the *Amolyntos*, the house of the emperor, as Teodoro Estudita puts it, and the one that produced the Misericordia, mentioned in the Theotokarion, took its figures from all the different Byzantine Glykophiloussa types…before arriving at Rizo's definitive model."

What gives them unity within this diversity and what allows us to designate them all Virgins of the Passion is precisely the idea of the Passion that exists in all of them. The differences relate to the forms in which this is expressed, which gradually mature. Therefore, despite what we have said with regard to the Eleusa, in this icon type, the holy Mother of God shows traces of very different Marian archetypes. Sometimes the inspiration appears to come from the Hodegetria, at other times from the Eleusa, and there are also examples that seem to derive from the Virgin Mother of God or the Virgin in Majesty. The most characteristic, however, are related to the Hodegetria and Eleusa types.

The figure of the child

The child appears to be the centre of the composition and the iconographic element most subject to variants. These may relate to his age, to which of the Virgin's arms supports him, to the halo (with or without a cross) that surrounds his head, to the colour, decoration and placement of the garments he is wearing, to the abbreviations, anagrams and literary texts that accompany him and to the movement of his head, his gaze, his arms, hands and feet.

The fundamental postures he presents are as follows: he reclines placidly or turns his head to one side as if contemplating an horrific vision; he clasps his Mother's hands or embraces her; he moves as if startled and the sandal of his foot (the right foot if he is on Mary's left arm) has fallen off and hangs by its laces, leaving the sole of his foot exposed.

Angels and archangels

These appear to the side of the composition or in the side panels of a triptych and are shown carrying the instruments of the Passion in their veiled hands. The signs that accompany the various figures enable us to identify who they represent. In the case of the archangels St Gabriel and St Michael, the former usually appears on the viewer's right and carries in his hands the cross and the crown of thorns or the nails, while the latter is placed on the left and carries the spear, the stick with the sponge and the vessel containing vinegar.

"Prior to the 14th century, medallions or figures of the archangels Gabriel and Michael never appear carrying the instruments of the Passion; they carry a messenger's staff, a sceptre or a disc. This provides a clue – together with the general style of the icon – to determining the period of the piece."[11]

The method of presentation includes the following variants:

- their presence or absence within the icon itself;

- the number: there are copies in which, in accordance with the ancient model, an angel only appears on one side of the composition, recalling the Macedonian model;

- the position and the dimensions;

- the age (adult or child) and type of figure (half, three-quarter or full-length);

- garments and colours;

- the instruments of the Passion they are carrying and which are characteristic of each kind (Greek or Latin cross, for example).

Titles, literary texts and abbreviations

There are examples in which these are entirely absent. This is frequently the case in examples from the former Yugoslavia, most of which date back to the 16th to 17th centuries. In the Arab world (Melchite icons), however, literary texts are usually translated into that language. Mirjana Tatic-Djuric identifies the following as being among the most common and significant Greek inscriptions found in icons of the Passion: *Cardiotissa, Amolyntos and Meter Theou (MP 0Y)*.

The designation *Cardiotissa* (of magnanimous heart) was particularly used in Crete. "There is a taste in Byzantine poetry for associating the immaculate conception of Mary with the title of *Amolyntos* (immaculate), a designation frequently used in post-Byzantine icons of the Passion." More than one of these may be attributed to Rizo of Candia, particularly where they also contain the literary text characteristic of his work. The inscription *Meter Theou (MP 0Y)*: Mother of God, appears on most icons, sometimes with one of the former titles or other less usual ones.

Reading the iconographic theme

Some scholars explain the theme of the Virgin of the Passion by saying that it is an attempt to represent "Jesus who, assailed by fear at the premonition of the tragic future that awaits him, turns away his head". But this movement does not appear in all the icons. Furthermore, María Soteriu, who supports this theory, states that the Mount Sinai Virgin of the Passion icon "combines the early type of the Eleusa Glykophiloussa with certain elements of the Virgin of the Passion and is therefore the missing link in the chain that connects these two iconographic types demonstrating clearly the messianic symbolism associated with the simple Glykophiloussa type".

Although Tatic-Djuric does not agree with this line of thought, he is, however, able to confirm that "The Byzantine artists have demonstrated clearly that the Glykophiloussa is not a simple type but an (iconographic) type considered and treated as a Virgin of the Passion. It is precisely this relationship with the Hodegetria and the Eleusa that justifies the importance accorded here to these iconographic themes. We need to refer back to them to achieve a better understanding. Within each type, the variants relate to the particular details of each school and each specific "legend".

3. THE CRETO-VENETIAN SCHOOL: IMPORTANCE, CHARACTERISTICS, DIFFUSION[12]

Early icons of the Virgin of the Passion are very rare compared with those of other iconographic themes. Only about one hundred of any great age (14th – 18th centuries) still survive today.[13] "A study of these immediately reveals that the majority of them were produced in the area of Crete, so much so that they could be described as typical of that region." According to the wording on the board in the church of St. Matthew in Rome, even the icon of the Virgin of the Passion known as Our Mother of Perpetual Help was stolen by a merchant from a famous Cretan shrine, where it was much venerated, and taken to Rome.[14] Moreover, "it is the liturgy of St Andrew of Crete (7th – 8th centuries) in honour of the Virgin that contains the most sublime praise of this theme".

Our Mother of Perpetual Help, 17th-18th century copy, with some variants, Redemptorist archive, Rome.

Therefore, "it can be said that this icon shows the presence of the Cretan school in other regions. Its presence was particularly strong in Venice from the 14th century onwards, and towards the end of the 15th century and throughout the 16th century it also spread into other geographical and cultural areas dependent on the Creto-Venetian region. It also seems that this image was especially venerated by Greek sailors who erected a number of chapels in her honour in coastal towns."[15]

As a result, the authors of and variants produced by this school, which were sometimes projected into other iconographic themes, deserve special attention. Also, given the importance of the Cretan school of iconography it is understandable that "the icon of the *Mother of God of the Passion* should become so widespread in the east in Byzantine times – there are numerous examples in the museums of Athens, Moscow, Crete, St Petersburg and in the Hellenic Institute in Venice (the most extensive collection of icons in Italy), and of course such icons are even more numerous in the churches of both east and west. Also in the west, this icon is venerated under the title of *Our Lady of Perpetual Help* in the shrine of the Redemptorists in the Via Merulana in Rome, and through them in particular, it has spread across every continent".[16]

In the *Museo de iconos rusos de la Casa Grande* in Torrejón de Ardoz (Madrid), "no. 45-D is a 'Holy Virgin' on metal that is an exact copy of the iconographic model that crystallised during the 15th to 16th centuries within Cretan painting. No detail is missing: the backwards movement of the head of Christ; the angels holding in their hands the instruments of the Passion; the sandal hanging loose

84

from Christ's foot. However, it is interesting that, after appearing in Russian iconography, this Cretan model should also avail itself of the protection and help afforded by the Russian bronze. There are some metal icons in the collection that reproduce this with no change whatever (nos. 292, 410, 423 and 829). The only differences between them are purely in the distribution of the enamel".[17]

Principal authors

Among the representatives of the Cretan school are some important authors whose icons of the Virgin of the Passion still survive. They include Andrea Rizo of Candia (1422-1499), Michele Damasceno (1574-1582), 16th-century anonymous artists in the tradition of Rizo, Emanuele Tzanfournaris (c. 1600), Emanuele Lambardos (works dating 1593 to 1647), Victor of Crete, Emanuele Tzane and others studied by M. Cattapan.[18]

Andrea Rizo of Candia

Of the icons of the Virgin of the Passion belonging to the school of Crete, six or seven are certainly the work of Andrea Rizo of Candia (1422-1499), the most famous of the *madonneri* (painters of Marian images), although others can also be attributed to him. His fondness for the theme is clear. The Bari icon carries the date 1451.

Virgin of the Passion with St Nicholas and St Blaise by Andrea Rizo of Candia, 15th century.

The variants introduced by Rizo of Candia and studied by M. Cattapan,[19] constitute the fundamental elements of the Cretan school as far as this type of icon is concerned. They can be summarised as follows:

- Hodegetria type, the basic icon type, in which the infant Jesus clasps with both hands the thumb of the right hand (the great hand) of the Hodegetria, is supported by the left and turns his head to the side on which the archangel Gabriel appears with the cross. The similarities with the icon of Our Mother of Perpetual Help are obvious, with the exception of certain of the elements described below.

- The face of the child is more rounded.

- The colours are reversed. Red is used for the Virgin's cloak and veil and blue for the tunic.

- White or grey is used for the tunic of the infant Jesus which also has "floral decorations (fleur-de-lis type), already present in the icon of San Fantino in Venice a century earlier, although this is also of Byzantine origin".

- Three stars (on the Virgin's forehead and front of her shoulders) with eight rays (two intersecting crosses) in which the fleur-de-lis is inserted, which also appears in the decoration of the veil (maphorion) as it falls over the Virgin's right shoulder, and on the child's tunic.

- The stippling of the halos.

- The frequent use of the title *Amolyntos* (Immaculate), together with the abbreviations *MP 0Y*.

- The Greek or Latin inscription below the figure of St Gabriel level with the child's face. Written in twelve-syllable verse, it reads:
  > *He who once filled the Immaculate with joy*
  > *now presents to her the symbols of the Passion;*
  > *and Christ, embodied in mortal flesh*
  > *and fearful of death, takes fright at their sight.*

- Lastly, the characteristic use of "the letter Y in the Greek abbreviations with the upper strokes terminating in a hook (uncinata) is sometimes more valuable than a signature".[20]

- But perhaps one of the most characteristic contributions of the Cretan School to the iconographic theme of the Virgin of the Passion is in fact the group of angels or archangels who carry the instruments of the Passion.

Two winged angels with the instruments of the Passion in their veiled hands are added to the composition formed by the fundamental iconographic themes derived from the Hodegetria type, with some of the movements shown by the infant Jesus, particularly in the Eleusa of the Passion. The element of winged angels in icons of the Virgin of the Passion is of Cretan origin and coincides with the presentation of these in certain representations of *The Descent of Christ into Limbo*, which most probably already existed in the second half of the 14th century or the first half of the 15th, although the side on which the angel carrying the cross appears differs in each of the compositions.

"This theme (Descent of Christ into Limbo), known for its widespread diffusion, is called the *Anastasis* or *Resurrection* by the Byzantines and

The Virgin of the Passion by Andrea Rizo of Candia exemplifying the particular characteristics of the artist as described in these pages.

The Descent into Limbo in the West. This representation, which alludes to the Resurrection, is based on the apocryphal account by Nicodemus ... Iconography on this subject is a constant of Byzantine art, although it shows some variants ... The iconography of this icon belongs to the type predominant in Daphni and Nea Moni in the 11th century, although it is characterised by variants arising from the art (of the period) of Paleologus (for example Sopocani, the mosaics of the Holy Apostles in Thessalonika and of the Privleptos of Mistra). The elegance of the rhythm of the composition and the harmonious gradation of colour might suggest that this refined icon constitutes an historical link between the Paleologus culture and the origins of Cretan art. We can therefore suggest a possible date for this work of between the end of the 14th century and the first half of the 15th century. The work was restored in 1958. The left part is badly damaged and the colour of

"Descent of Christ into Limbo",
Byzantine, 14th-15th century

the figure of Christ was removed during an earlier restoration".[21]

With regard to a work on the same theme by Michele Damasceno (dated between 1574 and 1582), Bandera Viani comments, "Christ, surrounded by the mandorla, is represented standing at the gates of Hades, which have been forcefully removed and placed again on earth in the form of a cross. With his right hand he gestures to Adam, who is kneeling, to approach" ... "Two small angels with the symbols of the Passion, floating over the scene, represent the Resurrection of Christ according to the apocryphal gospel of Nicodemus. The composition reflects the influence of traditional Byzantine painting ... with some variants which also reflect the creativity of the author".

These antecedents help to explain the need for an inscription below the figure of St Gabriel to accentuate the "portent of the Passion." This aspect was to occupy an important place in the iconographic theme of the angels with the instruments of the Passion in the new iconographic context into which it had been introduced. Did this mean that it would lose the allusion to the Resurrection of Christ? Could it not also be associated with the themes of the Virgin of the Passion deriving from the Eleusa and the Hodegetria and which do not contain this symbolism? In fact, where icons of the Passion are concerned, there is not usually an allusion to the Glorious Passion of Christ and, even less, any explicit iconographic allusion to the Resurrection. And yet, it was already there to some extent in the origins of this iconographic theme.

In the Queen Frederika of Greece collection there is an icon of the *Virgin of the Passion* with elements of the Cretan school (late 15th or early 16th century). In this "the Virgin supports the child on her *right* arm, while he turns towards the archangel Gabriel who carries the cross [on the viewer's left, as in icons of the Anastasis]. Unusually, it also shows the bare feet of the child, whereas in the type later established, the child's feet are covered up to his sandal by his tunic and he is supported on his Mother's left arm".[22] This icon bears the inscription "Amolyntos".

The catalogue of the *Museo delle Icone Bizantine e post Bizantine e Chiesa di San Giorgio dei Greci* (Venice)[23] describes some of the characteristics shown in works by the following artists:

- **Michele Damasceno**, who despite remaining faithful in the smallest detail to the iconographic model of the school of Rizo, displays his own artistic personality with "rounder faces, more delicate folds and a superior quality of light in the flesh tones"

- **An anonymous artist** of the 16th century, also after Rizo, in which "the abstract expression of the figures, the geometric treatment of the folds and the severe style" are very much in keeping with the master.

- **Emanuele Tzanfournaris**, "who offers us a stylised version, with a certain rigidity, characterised by a pronounced tendency towards the two dimensional"

- **Emanuele Lambardos**, the author of two well-known icons, one in the Mount Sinai monastery (1626) and the other in the church of the Philippians in Padua (1647)[24] (cf.p.80).

The Virgin of the Passion, "The Strastnaia", 17th-18th century, the Russian interpretation.

89

The Cretan model of the Virgin of the Passion also spread into Russia where it was known as the *Strastnaia*. The name comes from the liturgical term "Strastnoi" which refers to the Passion of Christ. Its feast is celebrated on 13 August and Easter Sunday. The most famous icon of this type in Russia, and the one associated with its veneration, is attributed to an iconographer called Gregory who, it is believed, copied it from the Cretan type in the 17th century with certain variants in the different iconographic elements. It is displayed in the town of Nishnij-Novgorod. It revealed its miraculous power in the healing of a woman in the village of Palitsy and, as a result of this, Prince Boris Michailowitsch had it moved to Lykov. In 1641 it was brought to Moscow by order of Tsar Alexander Michailowitsch and placed close to the Tverskie gate. Here, in 1654, the monastery of the Sisters of the Passion (Strastnyj Dewitschij Monastyri) was built in its honour, but this was destroyed in 1928.[25]

Modern representations of the Virgin of the Passion in Russia also rely on Our Mother of Perpetual Help. However, the theme is not restricted to these iconographic types. It is much broader and also includes very different expressions of the theme, which may help us to unravel the early significance of the Virgin of the Passion.[26]

The fact that these later began to take on the classical expression of the Cretan School, associated with the Hodegetria type in the Greek world, should not lead us to forget those associated explicitly with the different Eleusa types. These take us to a parallel tradition of the same iconographic theme and to a mutual influence in the development of this theme. It is therefore not surprising that the Strastnaia itself should be a rather late and somewhat uncommon theme in Russian iconography, as there were already other themes that carried the same meaning.

* * *

As we have seen in this chapter, the theme of the Virgin of the Passion is clearly related to the iconographic themes studied in the previous chapter and which include, in particular, the Hodegetria, the Eleusa and the Virgin in Majesty. But we should not lose sight of the fact that the icon of Our Mother of Perpetual Help is a significant example of the Virgin of the Passion associated with the Cretan School.

Notes to Chapter III

1 For a detailed study of this theme see M. Tatic-Djuric: *Iconographie de la Vierge de Passion. Genèse du dogme et des symboles*, in *De cultu mariano saeculis XII-XV.* Acta Congressus marioligici mariani internationalis Romae anno 1975 celebrati. Vol. VI. *De cultu mariano in litterarum studiis et in arte religiosa.* Rome, 1981, 135-169, with 21 graphic docs. 160-168.

2 P. Amato (ed.): *Imago Mariae.* Tesori d'arte della civiltà cristiana: Roma, Palazzo Venezia, 20 giugno – 2 ottobre 1988, Rome, 1988, 19.

3 Romano il Melode: *Inni*, Rome 1981, 183-184 and G. Gharib: *Le icone mariane: storia e culto*, Rome 1987, 214.

4 cf. Tatic-Djuric, p.137.

5 M. Cattapan: *Nuovi documenti riguardanti pittori cretesi dal 1300 al 1500*, in *Atti del II Congresso Internazionale Cristologico (1965)*, Vol. II, Athens, 1968, 39.

6 cf. E. Sendler: *La Vergine della Tenerezza.* Ed. pro ms. of *Plamia*, 71 (1987) 3-23, produced by the "Russia Ecumenica" Centre, 3, 5-7. Tatic-Djuric, 136-137.

7 cf. F. Ferrero: *Nuestra Señora del Perpetuo Socorro. Proceso histórico de una devoción mariana.* Madrid, 1966, 112, note 111.

8 M. Cattapan: *I pittori Andrea e Nicola Rizo da Candia.* In "Thesaurismata" (Venice), 10 (1973) 237-282, with 16 illustrations, 280, note 23.

9 On the influence of this literary source on other representations of this theme, cf. P. Amato (ed.): *Imago Mariae.* Tesori d'arte della civiltà cristiana: Roma, Palazzo Venetia, 20 giugno – 2 ottobre 1988, Rome, 1988, 19.

10 cf. Tatic-Djuric, pp.162-3.

11 E. Ros: *Iconografia mariana bizantino-rusa.* Barcelona, 1984, 39.

12 For the Cretan school of iconography see chapter I, 3C of this work in which we discuss the history of icons.

13 M. Cattapan: *Nuovi documenti riguardanti pittori cretesi dal 1300 al 1500* in *Atti del II Congresso Internazionale Cristologico (1965)*, Vol. II, Athens, 1968, 29. However, it should be noted that some examples have ceased to be considered as "icons of the Passion" as they do not include the "instruments" that allude to it. But if we bear in mind Tatic-Djuric's thesis, many examples of the Eleusa type would also be included in the icons of the Passion as a result of their history and the iconographic message they express.

14 M. Cattapan: *Nuovi documenti*, 30. For the text inscribed on the board at St Matthew's see Appendix I, p.131.

15 cf. P. Marangos: "El culto mariano popular en Grecia", in D.H. Manoir (ed.): *Maria. Etudes sur la Sainte Vierge*, Paris, 1952, V. IV, 821, quoted by E. Ros: *Iconografia mariana bizantino-rusa*, 39, note 13.

16 M. Donadeo: *Icone della Madre di Dio.* Brescia, 1987.

17 A. Bozhkov: *Informe general sobre el peritaje de los iconos y demás valores artísticos e históricos en la colección del señor Rafael Onieva Ariza en 'La Casa Grande',* Torrejón de Ardoz, Madrid, Nov-Dec, 1990, pro ms., 44.

18 cf. Tatic-Djuric, 166-167 and bibliography in M. Cattapan.

[19] cf. M. Cattapan: *I pittori Andrea e Nicola Rizo da Candia,* in "Thesaurismata" (Venice), 10 (1973) 237-282, with 16 illustrations and Tatic-Djuric, 165-168, to complete this theme.

[20] Cattapan: *I pittori Andrea e Nicola Rizo da Candia,* 266.

[21] cf. *Descendimiento al Limbo,* Anonymous 14th-15th century work, in M. C. Bandera Viani, 33-34, and 91-92

[22] E. Ros: *Iconografia mariana bizantino-rusa,* 39, note 11, which refers to the catalogue of the Exhibition of Byzantine Art, Athens, 1963, no. 220. Also on p. 40 E. Ros adds: "However, the typical, most beautiful icon, and that which includes all the characteristics already mentioned is the "Virgin of the Passion", the original of which can be admired in the Byzantine Museum of Athens, and whose author is the Cretan artist Juan Lambardos". It is shown in the catalogue as plate 5.

[23] cf. M. C. Bandera Viani: *Icone Bizantine e post Bizantine*. Musei d'Italia: Venezia, Museo delle Icone Bizantine e post Bizantine e Chiesa di San Giorgio dei Greci, Calderini, Bologna, 1988.

[24] For details of other artists cf. Tatic-Djuric, 165-168. On the example of Cretan origin belonging to the school of Rizo of Candia and preserved in the Recklinghausen Museum (Germany), cf. Gharib, *Le icone mariane,* 216-217, no. 20.

[25] For a history and description of this cf. C. M. Henze, *Mater de Perpetuo Succursu,* Bonn am Rhein, 1926, 20-21, photo 26; I. Bentchev, *Handbuch der Muttergottesikonen Russlands. Gnadenbilder-Legenden-Dartellungen,* Bonn, 1985, 103, 135, 135, illustr. 1, 85; M. Donadeo, *Icone mariane russe,* Brescia, 1988, 20.

[26] Massone-Manasse, 30. For the association of the Virgin of Vladimir with the theme of the Passion cf. E. Sendler: *La Vergine della Tenerezza,* ed. pro ms. of *Plamia,* 71 (1987), 3-23, produced by the "Russia Ecumenica" Centre, pp. 3, 5-7; Tatic-Djuric, 136-137.

The Mother of God before the sepulchre, 13th century. Russian icon with Persian influences. Theme of the Passion combined with the Virgin Praying.

CHAPTER IV

THE ICON OF OUR MOTHER
OF PERPETUAL HELP

1. DESCRIPTION OF THE ICONOGRAPHIC ELEMENTS

2. CHARACTERISTIC MATERIALS

3. AESTHETIC STRUCTURE OF THE ICONOGRAPHIC
   THEME

4. HISTORICAL PROVENANCE

Notes to Chapter IV

The church of Sant' Alfonso in Rome as it was until the restoration of the Shrine in 1994-5. In the centre is the original icon of Our Mother of Perpetual Help. Above this in the apse is a great mosaic of the Most Holy Redeemer, the Pantocrator, with the Virgin Mary and St Joseph. On the arch separating this from the nave is a painting of the Coronation of the Virgin Mary attended by angels and Redemptorist saints.

On entering the Redemptorist church of Sant' Alfonso in Rome, we are immediately struck by the mosaic of the Most Holy Redeemer above the sanctuary. However, as we approach the santuary, what really comes as a surprise is the presence of an icon of the Mother of God above and behind the altar, with all the aesthetic, iconographical, theological and historical richness associated with this type of image, above all, when it dates back as far as this one.

From its golden background arise four sacred figures: the Mother of God, Jesus Christ, and the archangels St Michael and St Gabriel with the instruments of the Passion, as we deduce from the Greek abbreviations accompanying them. If we continue to study more carefully the attitudes and symbolism that these figures reflect, we may wonder about the materials, the painting technique and the aesthetic structure of the icon. All this will help us better to understand its iconographic content, which is more complex than might at first appear. We will also want to know how this remarkable icon comes to be displayed for the veneration of the faithful in this church of Sant' Alfonso Maria de Liguori (1696-1787), the Founder of the Redemptorists.

1. DESCRIPTION OF THE ICONOGRAPHIC ELEMENTS

The icon of Our Mother of Perpetual Help is one of the most representative examples of the Hodegetria type Virgin of the Passion and of the Cretan School. The four figures referred to earlier present this iconographic theme to us, with the distinguishing features of the Roman icon. Let us examine the most interesting details each of these elements has to offer.

The Virgin

The Virgin appears as a half-figure, but in a standing posture. She is dressed in a red tunic with long, tight-fitting sleeves, a dark blue robe, and a shawl (maphorion)[1] of the same colour. This appears to have a green lining, while the golden colour of the folds, borders and decorations follows the style of the Cretan School. The

Central upper section detail of the icon of Our Mother of Perpetual Help, showing Mother and child, heads and hands typical of the Hodegetria.

shawl covers her head and falls over her arms and shoulders (which is how women used to wear them), but allows her celestial blue head covering or veil, with which she conceals her hair and part of her forehead, the red tunic at breast level and the cuff of her sleeve, to be seen. The neckline of the tunic has a gold border, with a brooch in the centre. In modern times, precious stones were added, but these were removed in the 1994 restoration. The right hand sleeve, in contrast, has two gold bands.[2]

In the centre of the head and on the shawl, is a star with eight straight rays; a little to the right, on the vertical axis of the picture, one can also see a cruciform star with a blue centre and gold highlight like the previous one.

The circular halo around her head has stippling and floral decoration, typical of the Cretan School. In 1867 metal crowns were added over this part of the Virgin's halo, and that of the child. It was these that were responsible for the very special style of this icon compared with other traditional icons of the Virgin of the Passion. Like the other precious stones, these crowns were also removed from the image during the last restoration.

Without these crowns, the gold of the painting and the figure of the Virgin seem to form the background from which the head of the child emerges, with its own cruciform halo, as if the Mother of God were the dawn and the star that reveal Christ to us. In the upper part of this space and perpendicular to the angels, the classic icon inscription – *MP OY: Meter Theou: Mother of God* – appears in red.

The Virgin, with her beautiful rounded head, recalling the Byzantine Marian type, turns slightly towards her left. With her right hand open (the large hand and long fingers of the Hodegetria), she receives the hands of the child, who clasps her thumb, while she supports him with her left hand. Her face conveys the gravity of images that receive veneration. Her gaze is sacred and profound. It is not directed towards her Son but towards whoever is contemplating her. Her large eyes with their pronounced eyebrows, her long nose, small mouth and gently pursed lips and the dark colour of her garments, give her whole figure a sacred grandeur that penetrates to the very heart of the viewer and of the mystery that she herself appears to contemplate as she gazes out.

The child Jesus

The child is shown with brown hair and childlike features and his whole body is visible. He is seated on the Virgin's left arm and with his hands he clings to the thumb of Mary's right hand, in the typical gesture of icons of the Passion, while his head is turned to his left. His look is not directed at the archangel Gabriel, but to a point outside the picture, situated to the right of the person contemplating the icon. The object of his gaze appears to be positioned symmetrically to the viewer. The archangel appears in the upper part of the composition, slightly inclined, and with a Greek cross above his veiled hands. At the foot of the cross there are four nails.

The child is dressed in a green, long-sleeved tunic with a red waistband and reddish mantle, revealing his arm and the left side of his body that is covered by the tunic, to be seen. The mantle and tunic are covered in lineal, gold folds.

He is wearing brown sandals with gold laces but the right sandal hangs loose and we are able to see the sole of his foot in a gesture which, with or without sandals, also appears in certain icons of the Hodegetria and Eleusa type that are not icons of the Passion: for example, in the Virgin of Vladimir (cf.p.60) and in the Tichwin Hodegetria (Tichvinskaja) type.

The face and the whole figure of the child seem to express a great serenity, despite the symbolism of the gestures of his feet and hands. To the right of his face are the abbreviations: *IC XC: Iesus Xristos: Jesus Christ*, and in his halo there is a cross outlined in red.

The Archangels Michael and Gabriel with the instruments of the glorious Passion.

The archangels with the instruments of the Passion

On a level with the Virgin's face and in the upper corners of the icon are two archangels. The one to the right of the viewer, is *O AP G : O Arkanguelos Gabriel: the Archangel Gabriel.* He is dressed in a tunic and mantle of purple with white shading. His hands are covered with the ends of the mantle, or with a veil of the same colour and he is holding a cross with three grey horizontal crossbeams with four black nails at its foot. His face is young (almost like that of a child), slightly elongated, his head is uncovered, and his dark brown hair falls behind his neck and down his back. He has flaming wings, of green and gold, and a circular halo, with stippling around its edges. He appears in profile, looking at the child, in an attitude of adoration and offering. The image is half-length. The archangel on the left is *O AP M : O Arkanguelos Mikael: the Archangel Michael.* He has a red tunic with a blue mantle or veil that covers his hands and nearly all of his body, except for his right arm. In his hands, he is holding a vase; protruding from this are a cane with a sponge and a lance. The other iconographic elements are similar to those of the Archangel Gabriel. His face is even more childlike and more similar to that of the child. His tunic is decorated in gold.

As in the Cretan School, the images of the archangels do not have the characteristics that classical iconography assigned to each of them. Nor do they define or motivate, the scene occupied by the Mother and child. Rather, they appear to be attending it, in an attitude of adoration and offering. Their looks converge on the head of Jesus. As a result, the instruments they present do not appear to announce a future event, capable of infusing terror, but rather as the glorious symbols of the Passion of Christ, equivalent to the glorious cross. Russian crosses always carry the inscription: "We bow before the cross and glorify your resurrection".[3] The attitude of the Virgin and child could be earlier than the theme of the Passion itself, as we have already suggested when commenting on the Eleusa and the Virgin of the Passion in general, although the archangels have been harmoniously integrated into the composition.

The Greek abbreviations

To identify the different figures just described, the icon carries a series of Greek abbreviations.

We will repeat them here, in the order in which they appear, by way of reminder:

MP 0Y = **Meter Theou: Mother of God** (in the two upper corners of the icon).

O AP M = **O Arkanguelos Mikael: the Archangel Michael** (above the archangel who is to the viewer's left).

O AP G = **O Arkanguelos Gabriel: the Archangel Gabriel** (above the angel on the right).

IC XC = **Iesus Xristos: Jesus Christ** (to the right of the child's head).

The metallic crowns

On 23 June 1867, on the Sunday before the feast of St John the Baptist, the icon of Our Mother of Perpetual Help was solemnly crowned by the Dean of the Vatican Chapter and crowns of gold and precious stones were put in place on the head of the Virgin and child. As time went by, more precious stones were added to the original ones. This was perhaps what caused the breaking of the wax seals on the golden screws that attached these crowns at the rear of the image. Later were added the stone in the eight ray star on the Virgin's forehead, and the diamond collar on the neckline of her tunic. The collar had a larger diamond in the centre with another eight on the sides: two to the right and six to the left of the viewer.

In order to protect the icon from further damage, the crowns and the jewels were removed from the icon when it was restored in the Vatican in 1994. These are now preserved in the safe deposit of Sant' Alfonso.

The icon of Our Mother of Perpetual Help showing the crowns and precious stones before the 1994 restoration.

Basic materials

The basic material is wood, prepared in accordance with the specific technique used for icons painted with distemper or tempera. The colours were added over gilt, except on areas of flesh, where it is not found. There are signs of incisions around the Virgin's head. The stippling of the halos, excellently preserved where the metallic crowns had been, was done with two round stamps.

Before the restoration of 1866, the panel had been reinforced at the back with two strips of wood, attached to it by thick iron nails, as was customary with icons to prevent them from bending. The effects of woodworm and other human intervention was also visible. Clearly visible were the grain of the wood; the strip attached to the four edges of the panel with 26 iron nails some 3 or 4 cm long; the stucco and other substances, with which holes in the wood have been filled; the ends of the 4 golden screws with which the crowns of the Virgin and child were fastened; the ends of another 3 silver screws fastening the brooch at the Virgin's neck; the remains of three wax seals, towards the middle of the picture, which appeared to have held some sign of authenticity.

The wood was in a good state of preservation, although it was a little bent or warped and some of the cracks were wide enough to allow light to pass through from one side of the panel to the other. Some of them predate the stucco, with which they were covered (possibly in 1964), and were already visible in photographs taken before the 1866 restoration.

Our Mother of Perpetual Help. Black and white photograph prior to the restoration of the icon in 1866.

2. RESTORATION OF THE ICON

The icon of Our Mother of Perpetual Help was restored during the first half of 1994 by technicians from the Vatican Museum. The sanctuary of the Church of Sant' Alfonso was also renovated at the same time. Work began early in 1994 and on 10 June, Fr Antonio Marrazzo, the Postulator General of the Redemptorists, who was responsible for the restoration of the icon and the shrine, presented the work which was nearly finished to the Redemptorist community in Rome.

The need for the Restoration

To the right and left of the image, the wood and gilt appeared to have been replaced, perhaps due to earlier deterioration. Also, there was evidence of restoration to the Virgin's face (the cheek, lower lip, left side of the shawl), the left side of the child's neck and in some other places. Yellowish colouring was seen over the whole of the image, due to the deterioration of the protective varnish. There were also some (few) areas of painting that appeared less consistent.

The whole image showed the restoration already carried out by 15 March 1866 by the Polish painter Leopold Nowotny (1822-1870), resident in Rome from 1847 and previously a disciple of Feuweich in Vienna, and of Schnorr in Munich.[4]

The urgent need for the recent restoration was highlighted in an article published in June 1992. "On October 12th 1990, when the icon of Our Mother of Perpetual Help was taken down for photographic purposes, it was discovered that both the painting and the panel on which it had been painted were in a grave state of deterioration." (Communicationes, No 92, June 25 1992) In a letter dated 27 June 1992, Father Juan M. Lasso de la Vega, the Superior General, wrote to the Redemptorist communities all over the world expressing the need for funds for the work of restoration of the icon, for the remodelling of its setting and the sanctuary of the church. Fr Lasso added, "We hope that this restoration project will eventually lead to a renewal of devotion to Our Mother of Perpetual Help".

The Restoration work

Before the actual restoration work began, the icon was examined in the Vatican Scientific Research Laboratory using the most modern scientific methods of analysis, including x-ray, infra-red, ultra-violet, carbon 14 dating. The restoration work was entrusted to Professor Maurizio de Luca, the Master of Restoration in the Vatican Museum. With the restoration work, the cracks in the woodwork have been removed and the holes made by nails filled in. However, it was a carefully conservative restoration in that no attempt was made to modernise the image or change its colours. Some specialist technicians who did not take part in the actual restoration later examined the finished work and approved of it.

The results of the carbon 14 dating analysis put the wood of the icon between the 14th and 15th centuries (1325-1480). On the other hand the artistic analysis tended to put the icon into the 18th Century because of the Cretan-Venetian influences that are evident in it. It has been suggested that we have here a unique copy, made in the 18th century, of a venerated icon of the 14th century. However, analysis does not reveal a more ancient image underneath. This has given rise to the suggestion that when the original colours began to fade and the wood to warp, it was decided to copy the precious original on to the back of the same wood.

Solemn Blessing
and Inauguration

On the Feast of Our Mother of Perpetual Help, 27 June 1995, the newly restored icon and the remodelled sanctuary were solemnly blessed and inaugurated by his Eminence Joseph Cardinal Bevilacqua, Archbishop of Philadelphia, to whom the church of Sant' Alfonso had been entrusted as his titular church in Rome.

The original icon of Our Mother of Perpetual Help following its restoration in 1994.

3. AESTHETIC STRUCTURE OF THE ICONOGRAPHIC THEME

What interests us is an examination of what the theme might signify for the reading of a specific icon.

Technical treatment

The technical treatment of perspective and of the faces of the Virgin and child, shows a highly evolved pictorial level. Although retaining the defining hardness of the outline (background and figure), it distances itself from the more primitive approach in its treatment of edges that used to be lineal with the outlines of the subject and zones of light being sharply defined (hard contrast). This new approach gives the figures greater relief and the transition from light to shade on their faces is handled more subtly, avoiding sharpness.

Aesthetic structure of the composition

As with every icon, the structure that concerns us here is something more than a simple design. It reflects a global concept of composition in which each one of the iconographic elements has its own place in accordance with the meaning it is called upon to express in the piece as a whole. Hence, in this icon too, the geometrical structure of the fundamental iconographic nuclei, the artistic interpretation of the design through which the iconographic theme is made explicit and the various symbolic elements that give expression to this theme, all form part of one whole.

The proportions of the original icon of Our Mother of Perpetual Help appear to be 2:3, in terms of the length of the base.[5] The square formed by the line running parallel to the base, is defined by a straight line that passes through the Virgin's head and above the heads of the archangels. The centre of this square (that is also the centre of its central parallel) coincides with the hands of Jesus and Mary, whereas the centre of the upper section is situated almost in the centre of the halos around the Virgin's head.

When establishing the geometrical lines of the icon we need to take into account the alterations there may have been to the edges and, having done this, we find that the following elements are along the vertical axis: the star in the form of a cross, the eye and mouth of the Virgin; the meeting point of the Virgin's right

Aesthetic and geometric structure of the icon of Our Mother of Perpetual Help.

hand with the hands of the child; and the left foot of Jesus himself. Also very close to the same vertical axis, is the brooch that adorns the neckline of the Virgin's tunic.

The proportions of the face and head of the Virgin and child, appear to be those traditional to Byzantine icons. Here the artist has made use of the space corresponding to the length of the Virgin's nose. Using this he has traced three circles: the smallest contains the eyes and nose; the second, the head; and the third, the halo. The central point is at the start of the nose, between the two eyes, in the centre of the head, which is, in turn, the seat of wisdom.[6]

However, to understand the geometric structure of the icon, we need to bear in mind the movement in the heads of the Virgin and child and the various straight lines and circles that can be drawn from the different geometrical points of the original composition. Taking this into account, it is perhaps possible to discover a greater harmony in this combination of iconographic elements.

We will leave this analysis to the specialists and here simply put forward a hypothesis on interpretation and contemplation. We believe, in fact, that the icon has been created to be contemplated at a certain distance to the left of the viewer, and at an angle of some 45 degrees in relation to the geometric centre of the icon's square, located, as we have already said, at the meeting point of the hands of Jesus and Mary. In practice this means from the angle of the bottom right-hand corner.

Viewed thus, all the elements that comprise it acquire a greater harmony and are seen in stronger relief. Furthermore, the aesthetic centre of the composition moves to the head of the child and attention falls on the cross of his halo as though reminding us of the glorious cross – the removal of the metallic crown has allowed this to be revealed.[7]

This impression is reinforced if we take into account the geometric structure of the composition. This viewpoint, in fact, coincides with the transverse axis of the icon's square, in which are found (with the approximations already mentioned): the arm and hand of the Hodegetria; the hands, the face and the anagrams of Christ; the figure of the Archangel Gabriel with the cross; and even the characteristic inscription found on this icon type. In fact, the central theme of Hodegetria type icons of the Passion and of the Cretan School. Is there also an intention to emphasise its relation to the theme of the Annunciation?

The other iconographic nucleus is found in the geometric centre of the upper section and presents the face of the Theotokos, typical of "icons of the "motherhood" of Mary. In these, "the child is normally situated below the upper line of the square, forming part of the base. In Hodegetrian Virgins (dating from the late 14th century), the centre is also found above this line; but in order to place the two main figures in correct balance, the symmetrical axis has been moved towards the left. This type of composition has the disadvantage of creating an overly large space in the two upper corners of the picture. This is one of the reasons why the Virgin's halo (in some examples) extends beyond the frame. This helps to reduce the empty space and the figure appears closer to the viewer, almost appearing to emerge from the picture".[8]

In our icon, the empty space is also offset by the two images of the archangels who are situated precisely in the upper corners of the square and positioned symmetrically with the Virgin's face. As a result, the basal square has as its centre the right hand of the Mother (Hodegetria) and is dominated by the iconographic nuclei of the hands and head of the child, while the Virgin's face lies at the centre of the upper section.

Diagonal reading of the icon, with its three defining elements: the hands, the head of the child and the angel.

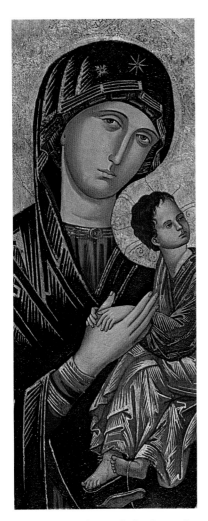

Vertical reading of the icon, in which the sacred grandeur of the Mother of God stands out, yet remains imbued with human warmth.

One could also make further, more or less plausible, geometric correlations. For example, if we look at the archangels in their geometric relation with the figure of the child, they acquire, within the iconographic square as a whole, an aesthetic harmony that is not so clearly perceived when they are contemplated in relation to the image of the Mother. And from this point of view, it is perhaps possible to see them not simply as an addition but as making the theme of the Passion explicit also in structural terms, something that does not happen in all icons that bear this name.

Finally, the face of the Virgin, by dominating the upper part of the composition, gives, an aesthetic consistency not easy to explain, to the figure of Mary as a whole. Compared with the "levity" that the iconographic elements related to the image of the child suggest, we have the strength, weight and sacred grandeur inspired by the Mother of God. This is what we experience when we contemplate this image: the face and gaze of Mary, the volume that perspective gives to her whole body, the darkness of the colours and the grandeur of her hands. In this icon, the Mother of God reflects more the humanity through which the Word was made flesh, than the femininity of the woman chosen to be his mother. Her sacred grandeur has the weight of humanity. The levity and luminosity of Christ and of the angelic spirits stand out against her and against the gilding of the icon.

4. HISTORICAL PROVENANCE

The iconographic theme and the artistic style of the icon that we have just described take us back to the Cretan School of iconography. However, in order to explain how this icon came to be in the church of Sant' Alfonso in Rome we need to look at the history, tradition and legend that relate to it.

The icon of Our Mother of Perpetual Help in Rome

According to a 16th century Roman tradition, this image of the Virgin was removed from Crete by a merchant from that island. He hid the image, which had performed many miracles in a church on the island, among his baggage and left Crete on board ship. A fearsome storm arose and it was only through divine providence that he reached his port of destination. A year later he arrived in Rome, still with the image in his possession.

Falling gravely ill, he sought out a Roman friend to look after him. On his deathbed he revealed the secret of the image to this friend, asking him to place it in a church. His friend promised to do this, but because of opposition from his wife, he also died without fulfilling the promise.

Finally, the Holy Virgin appeared to the six-year old daughter of this Roman family, and told her to tell her mother and grandfather that the image of *Saint Mary of Perpetual Help* should be placed between the great Basilicas of St Mary Major and St John Lateran, in the church there dedicated to the apostle St Matthew.

After a number of difficulties "the mother obeyed and, having informed the friars of Saint Augustine at this church ... this image of the most glorious Virgin was placed in the church of St Matthew the Apostle on 27 March 1499". There it remained for almost three hundred years.

In 1798 or 1799, the church and part of the monastery was destroyed. A few Augustinian Fathers remained there until 1801. When religious life became impossible for them, some returned to Ireland (from 1739 the church and the convent annexed to it, were entrusted to Irish Augustinians as the first training centre for the province in Rome), others went to foundations in America, while the majority moved to the church and monastery of S. Eusebio, near to St Matthew. The image of Our Mother of Perpetual Help went with them.

In 1819, the Irish Augustinians moved to the church of S. Maria in Posterula, next to the Tiber and now close to the Umberto I Bridge, and took the St Matthew Virgin with them. As Our Lady of Grace was venerated in that church, the new image was placed in a private chapel of the convent, where it remained, virtually unknown, until 1865. Its history had been forgotten. Only Brother Augustine Orsetti, a survivor from St Matthew's, continued to encourage devotion to the image.

A boy called Michele Marchi often attended the church of S. Maria in Posterula and he became a great friend of Brother Augustine. One day, when Michele had become a Redemptorist, he wrote down what the brother had told him:

"This good brother would repeat to me, always with a certain air of mystery and anxiety, particularly in 1850 and 1851, these very words: 'You know, friend Michael, the St Matthew Madonna is the one up there in the chapel: do not forget that … It is true. It is true. Do you understand dear Michael? It was miraculous!' At that time this brother had almost completely lost his sight."

"With regard to this venerated image – the St Matthew Madonna, known as the Perpetual Help – that from the time of my childhood until I entered the Congregation (of the Most Holy Redeemer) I had seen it on the altar of the private chapel of the college of the Augustinian Fathers of the Province of Ireland, known as S. Maria in Posterula … unvenerated, without decoration of any kind and almost abandoned, without even a lamp to illuminate it and usually covered in dust. Often when I assisted there at Mass I would look at it repeatedly and with great attention."

Brother Augustine died in 1853, at the age of 86, without seeing his wish fulfilled that the icon of the Virgin of Perpetual Help might be displayed again for public devotion.

The discovery of the icon

On 31 January 1855, the Redemptorists purchased the Villa Caserta from the Gaetani family, in order to transform it into the Generalate House for the Congregation in Rome. In the area of this property were the sites of the church and convent of St Matthew. Without realising it, they had bought precisely the land that, many years before, the Virgin had chosen for her shrine between St Mary Major and St John Lateran.

On 4 May 1855, they began construction of a church to the Most Holy Redeemer, in honour of St Alphonsus de Liguori. It was consecrated on 3 May 1859.

On 24 December 1855, the novitiate of the Redemptorists in Rome was opened in this house. Among the novices, was Michele Marchi. Once he had become a professed and ordained priest, he was to serve in this community.

The Redemptorists were naturally interested in any information relating to their new property. On 7 February 1863, for example, they were surprised by the sermon given by a famous Jesuit preacher, Fr Francesco Blosi, in the no less famous church of Gesù (Jesus), about an image of Mary that "was in the church of *San Matteo in Merulana* and was known by the title of the *Madonna de San Matteo* and more correctly, by that of the *Perpetual Help*". On another occasion, "the chronicler of the house of Sant' Alfonso, while examining the work of certain authors with respect to Roman antiquities, found some information concerning the church of St Matthew. This included the fact that in that church (situated precisely in the convent garden), there was an ancient image of the Mother of God, held in great veneration and famous for the miracles it performed".

The conclusion was still to come and it explains the importance of Fr Marchi in the history of this icon. "Having related this to his fellow brothers and having begun to discuss where the miraculous image could be found, Fr Marchi told them what he had heard from Brother Augustine Orsetti, declaring that he had often seen this image and that he knew very well where it was."

The delivery of the icon to the Redemptorists

With this, the Redemptorists' interest in knowing more about the icon grew. Once they knew its history, the Superior General, Fr Nicholas Mauron, presented a report to the Pope, asking that the image of Perpetual Help be placed in the new church erected in honour of St Alphonsus, near to where the church of St Matthew had stood. Pius IX, who had as his motto always to act to the greater honour of Mary Most Holy, agreed to this request and, on the back of the report, he wrote in his own hand:

11 December 1865

The Cardinal Prefect of Propaganda will summon the Superior of the community of Santa Maria in Posterula and will tell him that it is our wish that the image of the Most Holy Mary, to which this report relates, should return to its position between St John Lateran and St Mary Major; and that the Liguorians (the Redemptorists) should provide the community with another suitable painting in its place.

Copy of the icon of Our Mother of Perpetual Help, Redemptorist archive, Rome.
This image was given to Pope Pius IX by Fr Nicholas Mauron, the Redemptorist Superior
General, on 21 April 1866.

According to tradition, it was also then that the Pope spoke these words to Fr General: "Make her known throughout the world".

On 19 January 1866, Fr Michele Marchi (a privileged witness of its history) and Fr Ernesto Bresciani (in charge of the church of Sant' Alfonso) went to S. Maria in Posterula to collect the sought after icon of Our Mother of Perpetual Help.

On 26 April 1866, after the appropriate restoration, carried out by the Polish painter Leopold Nowotny, it was again placed on display, just as we know it today, for public veneration in the church of Sant' Alfonso on the Esquiline hill.

The universal spread of the icon and its devotion

Since then, devotion to the icon has continued to grow. Copies of the icon that began to circulate from Rome throughout the world have contributed to this. On 21 April 1866, the Superior General of the Redemptorists gave one as a gift to Pope Pius IX. According to tradition, it was on the 5th of May the following year, when he made a personal visit to the church of Sant' Alfonso and prayed before the icon, that the Pope said to the Fr General: "How beautiful it is; I prefer it to the one you have given me!… Surely, you will not refuse to help your poor Pope" That copy is preserved today in the archives of the Generalate House of the Redemptorists, in Rome. It is reproduced on page 111.

The fact that the Redemptorists made this the Marian image of their Congregation also had a decisive influence on the spread of devotion to Our Mother of Perpetual Help. This explains, for example, its presence in so many churches throughout the world: it frequently serves as a memorial to the popular missions preached by the Redemptorists.

In recognition of the popular devotion it was receiving in Rome, on 23 June 1867 (the Sunday before the feast of John the Baptist), the image of Our Mother of Perpetual Help was solemnly crowned by the Dean of the Vatican Chapter. It was a solemn and official recognition of the Marian icon retrieved from obscurity. Such a coronation was reserved only for religious images that had been venerated over a long period of time and which had been instruments of extraordinary grace for the faithful.

Each of the crowns was set with twenty-six precious stones. That of the Virgin had nine millefiori, eight amethysts, five aquamarines and four emeralds. That of the child was set with thirteen garnets, eight pearls, three emeralds and two topazes. At this coronation, the Superior General of the Redemptorists solemnly swore that these crowns would never be removed from the image. Later, the necklace was added and more precious stones.

Members of the eastern Church saw this coronation as an ecumenical gesture. The Dean of the Vatican Chapter, who conducted the coronation, held the title of Patriarch of Constantinople, and the image itself recalled eastern icons.

On 23 May 1871, the Pious Union of Our Lady of Perpetual Help was established in the church of Sant' Alfonso in Rome, under the patronage of St Alphonsus, and the image of the Virgin was placed in the new altarpiece of the high altar. This was replaced in 1966, and again at the restoration in 1994. The Archconfraternity of Our Lady of Perpetual Help and of St Alphonsus Maria de Liguori was formed on 31 March 1876.

The liturgical feast of the Blessed Virgin Mary with the title of Perpetual Help was established, with its own office and mass, on 18 May 1876. The day of celebration was set as the Sunday before the feast of St John the Baptist, the day on which the 1867 coronation had taken place. In 1913 the feast was moved to 27th June. However, in 1916 it returned to the Sunday before the 24th June but finally, on the 14th May 1975, the celebration of the feast went back to the 27th June.

The 25th December 1878 saw the birth of the **Suplica Perpetua** in Santiago in Chile. The first shrine in honour of Our Mother of Perpetual Help at the new "Rock" church in St Louis, Missouri, was blessed in 1873. Then in 1922 the preaching of Fr Andrew Browne began to draw immense crowds to "The Rock" week by week. In 1928 the **Perpetual Novena** in honour of Our Mother of Perpetual Help officially began. From the church of St Alphonsus ("The Rock Church") in the city of St Louis in the United States of America this devotion would spread around the world.

The Shrine of Our Mother of Perpetual Help in "The Rock" Church, St Louis, MO, USA.

These were the first steps in the great dissemination around the world of the icon of Our Mother of Perpetual Help from 1866 onwards and which helps to explain the importance that it has today.

Iconographic repercussions of this process

The return of the icon of Our Mother of Perpetual Help to public devotion in Rome in 1866, led, in the first instance, to its artistic restoration and later, to its universal dissemination, particularly through the churches, popular missions and Marian preaching of the Redemptorists. In order to respond to the needs of this dissemination, "authentic copies" began to be made which, as soon as they had "touched the original" in Rome and often been "blessed" and "enriched with indulgences" by the Pope, were sent to Redemptorist communities and to centres of great devotion. The general archive of the congregation keeps a "register" of such shipments and of the documents by which indulgences were granted (Papal Rescripts).[9]

At the beginning, these copies were made by artists resident in Rome. Very soon, these proved insufficient, due to the number required and the economic cost. This led to the production of printed copies. Among these was a black and white photograph of the original, taken before its restoration in 1866.[10] As a result, very soon artistic copies and photographic reproductions or prints of the icon in a wide variety of different forms and sizes began to be produced.

But this was not sufficient either. As devotion and veneration spread, artists and publishers emerged who took up the task of disseminating the image in accordance with the popular tastes and needs of each region and period.

During this process, the image began to lose some of the aesthetic features associated with icons: its sacred quality and religious primitivism; the faithfulness to the "Marian portrait" derived from the Hodegetria; the inverse perspective; the psychology of colour, as the image became gradually more humanised and regionalised. The fundamental symbolic elements of the Virgin of the Passion were preserved, but it was not a question of producing "authentic copies" of the original icon. These, often, "did not please people", who preferred the "pious" reproductions, in a wide variety of technical and artistic styles: painting, sculpture, mosaic, stained-glass windows, enamel, precious metals, engraving, photography, lithography, chrome-lithography, prints, and the like.

The faithful continued, in their own way, to see a fundamental Christian theme in such images: that of the Mother of God, associated with the culminating moment of the salvation of people and of the universe, in Christ Jesus, truly God and Man. Present at the mystery of the incarnation, life, passion and death of Christ, the Mother of the Saviour became a path and guide (the Hodegetria) of he who is the supreme "way, the truth and the life". However, these artistic or popular reproductions of the fundamental symbolism embodied in the icon, caused it to lose the aesthetic, psychological and technical and artistic qualities that made it what it was.

Precisely because of this, the restoration of an icon as popular as that of Our Mother of Perpetual Help can be of significant service to universal Marian piety and to specialists in Christian iconography. However, as we achieve this, we must not lose sight of its link with Marian intercession and popular devotion to the Mother of God.

Stained glass window at the church of Our Lady of Perpetual Help in Kansas City, MO, USA.

Notes to Chapter IV

[1] On other occasions and in common with other authors, we have used the term "short cape". We believe that this is inappropriate, given the real meaning of the terms. This short cape, in fact, was a "garment that women wore about neck and over the shoulders for protection or adornment". It could also be worn over the cape or mantle. The shawl, on the other hand, was used by women to cover their heads and generally had decorations of tulle or embroidery (J. Casares). It therefore corresponds to the Greek "maphorion": a veil that covered the head and shoulders. According to tradition, that of the Virgin was preserved in Blaquernas.

[2] The Virgin's garments are shown much more clearly in the full length Hodegetrias.

[3] A. Bozhkov: Informe general sobre el peritaje de los iconos y demás valores artíscos e históricos en la colección del señor Rafael Onieva Ariza en "La Casa Grande" Torrejón de Ardoz, Madrid, Nov-Dec., 1990, pro ms., 49.

[4] cf. F. Ferrero: Nuestra Señora del Perpetuo Socorro. Proceso histórico de una devoción mariana, Madrid, 1966, 118-119, 187.

[5] Throughout this section there is the risk of inaccuracy in the exact measurements of the icon, given the changes that may have occurred to the edges. It is also difficult to draw on known reproductions, because often they do not respect the proportions of the original. As a result, in the description that follows, we cannot provide a description of the image based on millimetres.

[6] cf. E. Sendler, *L'icona*, 108-112.

[7] In a 17th-18th century copy, the cruciform halo has purple gilt (reddish gold, as though to indicate the flame of the Holy Spirit), which serves to highlight further the divinity of the Lord and the importance of this iconographic element.

[8] E. Sendler: *L'icona immagine dell'invisible. Elementi di teologia, estetica e tecnica (Theological, aesthetic and technical elements)*, Edizioni Paoline, Cinisello Balsamo, 1985, 90. The author refers to the geometric distribution artists had to give on the icon surface to achieve "the forms corresponding to the golden number" of the proportions (ib. 85), that can be found in any classical icon.

[9] cf. AGHR, PS, VI. Expeditio Imaginum authenticarum.

[10] cf. *AGHR, PS, I. Imagines B. M. V. de Perpetuo Succursu*, I, 1. See page 100 for the reproduction of a black and white photograph taken before restoration in 1866.

CHAPTER V

RE-READING THE ICON OF
OUR MOTHER OF PERPETUAL HELP

T he icon of Our Mother of Perpetual Help is an example of one of the more recent Marian iconographic themes. Therefore, if we want to discover the message it carries we need to read it afresh in the light of the study of iconography just presented.

What is the message that Our Mother of Perpetual Help conveys to those who contemplate the image carefully?

The icon of Our Mother of Perpetual Help offers all of the following –

- A portrait of the *Theotokos* or Mother of God,
- of the Hodegetria-Eleusa type,
- to which the iconographer has added the instruments of Christ's glorious Passion
- carried by the archangels Michael and Gabriel in their veiled hands.
- The stars on the forehead of the Mother of God,
- the great hands of Mary,
- the current title of the icon: *Our Mother of Perpetual Help*,
- the attitude of Christ in the arms of his Mother,
- and the presence of the instruments of the Passion in the configuration of the icon,
- invite us to remember, to contemplate and experience the great mystery of salvation in Christ that begins with the Incarnation and culminates in the Passion, Death and Resurrection of the Son of God and to which Mary is indivisibly linked.

1. ICONOGRAPHIC AND THEOLOGICAL SYNTHESIS OF THE HODEGETRIA AND THE ELEUSA

When embarking on the iconographic study which this response to our question involves, it is important to bear in mind that the icon does not tell a story, rather it presents a theological theme with symbolic images. Everything in these is arranged in accordance with the criterion of composition. For example, the association of the archangels with the memory of events that took place in different periods and in diverse circumstances (the Annunciation, the divine Motherhood of Mary, the Presentation of Jesus in the temple, the Crucifixion, the Death of Our Lord on the

Cross, the Resurrection, biblical allusions to the mission of the archangels Michael and Gabriel, etc.) evokes, in a single moment, the profound meaning of all these historical and theological events.[1]

It is this that makes the icon of Our Mother of Perpetual Help a world of symbols and messages, transforming it, at the same time, into an inexhaustible source of aesthetic and religious contemplation. It is not surprising, therefore, that in contemplation of this icon one should move easily from artistic admiration to authentic Christian prayer, the purpose for which it was created.

This is partly due to the fact that the original icon of Our Mother of Perpetual Help was written by the iconographer at a time when the Christian art of symbols was reaching the end of its creative process. As a result it embraces, becomes a synthesis of, the fundamental elements of earlier Marian iconography. Moreover, by accentuating in the Virgin of the Passion (so much associated with the iconographic type of the Eleusa) those elements originating in the Hodegetria type, it preserves the sacred quality and the Christocentric character of this type of icon, without, however, losing the theological and maternal message of the Eleusa. On the contrary, it becomes an iconographic and theological synthesis of both types and themes.

The image of the Virgin's face invites us to contemplate the teaching of the first councils of the Church on the Theotokos, the Mother of God.

2. THE FACE OF MARY: A PORTRAIT OF THE MOTHER OF GOD

The type of image used by the iconographer to paint the icon of Our Mother of Perpetual Help, corresponds to portraits of the Mother of God. This is clear from the composition as a whole and from the Greek abbreviations that refer specifically to the *Theotokos* of the Councils of Nicaea (325), Ephesus (431) and Chalcedon (451)[2] and the *Virgin Mother of God* of the fundamental themes of Marian iconography: Mary, the Virgin Mother of the Promised Messiah (2ⁿᵈ to 3ʳᵈ centuries), Mary, Mother of God and Empress (4ᵗʰ century), Mary, Mother of God Praying (4ᵗʰ century), Mary, Mother of God Hodegetria (5ᵗʰ century) and Mary, Mother of God Eleusa (11ᵗʰ century).[3] For precisely this reason, the iconography of Our Mother of Perpetual Help remains incomprehensible if one fails to take into account the icons of the Virgin of the Passion and the relationship between these and earlier iconographic themes.

3. THE PANTOCRATOR AND THE THEOTOKOS

This leads us to two other iconographic themes fundamental to the reading of Christological and Marian icons: the Pantocrator and the Theotokos. Both these themes must be kept in mind when we use this type of icon for worship and prayer. And, in a certain way, the icon of Perpetual Help invites us to do just this by highlighting two central theological and iconographic themes: Jesus Christ, truly God and truly man, and the Immaculate Mother of God (Amolyntos and Theotokos).

In the Pantocrator or Almighty we are invited to contemplate the mystery of Christ in accordance with the Christological doctrine of the Councils mentioned above. Therefore this theme does not simply represent one of his two natures but his very person, in which human and divine nature are combined.

The image of Christ, the Pantocrator, invites contemplation on the teaching of the first Councils of the Church on the mystery of Christ, divine and human. 14ᵗʰ century Russian icon.

The true Son of God, he is also the Son of Man. Consubstantial with the Father through his divinity, he also shares genuinely in human nature through his humanity. Hence, the image of Jesus Christ, Pantocrator, seeks to show us the mystery of the Incarnation to which the Theotokos is indivisibly linked.[4]

Theotokos or Mother of God, is the title discussed and proclaimed at the Council of Ephesus (431) and given to Mary to indicate her divine maternity in its own right, following the doctrine of St Cyril against Nestor. Within the context of Christological disputes this is one of the key categories to explain the union of divine and human nature in the mystery of the Incarnation.[5]

"Since Ephesus, the divine motherhood of Mary has constituted a unique title of nobility and glory for the mother of the Word made flesh. To recognise Mary as the mother of God means, in fact, to profess that Jesus, the carpenter from Nazareth who was crucified, the son of Mary through his human birth, is the Son of God and God himself."[6]

The iconography that began to develop after Ephesus to express this doctrine has already been discussed in our study of Marian iconographic archetypes. In the icon of Our Mother of Perpetual Help, the theme of the Eleusa has been accentuated by giving full symbolic expression to the theme of the Passion.

4. THE INSTRUMENTS OF THE GLORIOUS PASSION OF CHRIST

The instruments of the Passion, combined with the Theotokos and aesthetically related to the figure of Christ, are an explicit evocation of the mystery of the Incarnation, Passion, Death and Resurrection of Christ. "All the images that represent Christ during his time on earth refer to the Incarnation. This is particularly true of the images of his death on the cross as Christ's death had always figured among the essential proofs of his genuine incarnation. Only at the start of the Middle Ages did painters begin to use the theme to recall the reality of Christ's death." Until then their approach had been, above all, "To show his glory, his victory over death (as a symbol of the Resurrection) and the universality of salvation by means of the cross, etc."[7]

Christ contemplates the Cross of Victory.

The same could be said of the instruments of the Passion: they do not appear as signs of Christ's execution at Calvary but as a memorial to his glorious Passion. Therefore, they already have the sacred value conferred on them by their association with the mystery of the Passion, Death and Resurrection of Christ. With these instruments in their hands the angels accompany him in his descent to the place of the dead heralding the triumph over death.

5. THE STAR ON THE VIRGIN'S FOREHEAD

To understand the eight-pointed star that appears on the Virgin's forehead, we need to refer back to the meaning this symbol had in ancient Christian iconography. It could be said to replace "the ray of light, the hand of the Father who blesses from on high or the dove that descends bathed in light". Each of these symbolises the grace that descends upon the Mother of God.

The star normally appears on images of Mary with the child, where such iconographic motifs signify the coming Incarnation of Christ as announced by a prophet (as is the case in the catacomb of Priscilla). It also appears in the Nativity where it indicates the acknowledgement of the Incarnation by the Magi and the shepherds.

In cases such as these, Christian painters took their inspiration from the gospel text that refers to the star of Bethlehem. According to the Akathistos hymn (Od. 9), however, it is not a star that guides the faithful, as once guided the Magi, but the Virgin Mary.

The two symbolic stars on the head of Our Mother of Perpetual Help.

The placing of the star on the Virgin in scenes that do not show the Nativity or the Adoration of the Magi, was suggested to artists by pagan iconography in which the star was seen by all as the symbol of the divine presence or astral intercession on which such characters as dioscuri, heroes, emperors and other individuals remembered after death, could depend.[8]

In more recent periods, the use of the star began to take on various forms with very different symbolic allusions. Thus, the three stars (one on the forehead and two on the shoulders) that appear on some icons of the Virgin may be an allusion to the Holy Trinity. The other star that adorns the Virgin's head on the vertical axis of the icon may be a recollection of this distribution. Its cruciform shape, however, suggests one of its many other meanings, which include purity, light, the star of the sea, as can be found in the Akathistos hymn.

6. THE GREAT HANDS OF THE MOTHER OF GOD

In the icon of Our Mother of Perpetual Help, as in all Marian icons that derive from the Hodegetria, Mary's hands have a highly symbolic significance.

In her left hand the Virgin holds the hand of he who holds the universe in his hand and whom neither heaven nor earth can contain. The words of the Akathistos hymn read as follows:

The hands of Mother and child in the icon.

"He who sits in glory, on the throne of Divinity, Jesus, the Supreme God, came in a veil of cloud, into the arms of the Immaculate, and brought salvation to those who cried out, 'Glory, O Christ, to your power'" (Od. 4).

"Hail to you who bear he who sustains all" (Od. 1). "Hail to you, the seat of God, the Infinite one; hail to you, the portal of the sacred mystery … Hail, to this throne more holy than that of the cherubim; hail seat more beautiful than that of the seraphim" (Od. 15).

"The Magi contemplated the supreme work of man in the arms of his Mother and knowing him to be the Lord, despite his lowly aspect, immediately presented to him their gifts, saying to the fortunate Mother: Hail" (Od. 9).

Mary's right hand is, above all, the Hodegetria hand, that is to say, the hand of she who shows the path to Christ, who is the Way, the Truth and the Life. Therefore, as in the wedding feast at Cana, she appears to say to believers: "Do whatever he tells you" (Jn 2:5).

"Mary bows to the will of Jesus and directs us to him. Her Son is the focus of her life, her centre and her reason for being. With these words spoken by Mary in Cana, the new Christian existence begins and the trajectory of the Messianic community is laid out. The Virgin's intervention at the wedding feast places her not only before Jesus to entreat him to perform a miracle, but also before his servants and the first disciples to guide their steps towards the messianic Bridegroom. In a scene in which Mary appears at first sight as the main protagonist, attention is in fact drawn to Jesus, who becomes the real focus.

"The words spoken by Mary in Cana recall the formulas used by the people of Israel to ratify the Alliance (cf. Ex 19:8; 24, 3-7; Dt 5:27) or to renew commitments made (cf. Jos 24:24; Est 10:12; Ne 5:12). They are, above all, an echo of the words of the Father in the theophany of Tabor: 'Listen to him' (Mt 17:5). These formulas suppose and imply recognition of the sovereignty of God (cf. Paul VI, *Marialis Cultus*, n. 57).

"John the Evangelist places the story of Cana 'three days after' the calling of Philip and Nathaniel, which followed that of Andrew, Simon, James and John. They were the first to be summoned by Jesus, and Mary points out to them the path they should follow: "Do whatever he tells you". This refrain opens the public life of Jesus, and the apostles are invited to be the first to follow it. Doubtless Mary had learned and practised this in the many years she lived with Jesus in Nazareth. When this advice comes from her lips it demonstrates to us the inner path she follows in her life.

"Mary leads us to Jesus. And Jesus is to be found close to Mary. Throughout the mystery of the Virgin we also find her Son: from the Incarnation to Calvary, from the Resurrection to Pentecost. Mary appears before us, in the words of the 2nd Vatican Council, as she who 'devoted herself totally, as a handmaid of the Lord, to the person and work of her Son, under him and with him, serving the mystery of redemption, by the grace of Almighty God' (LG, 56). 'She prompts the faithful to come to her Son, to his sacrifice and to the love of the Father' (LG, 65). Christian teaching is united in inviting us to find harmony with Mary if we wish to be in harmony with her Son, because Mary is our teacher in the 'school of Jesus', she is the 'perfect Christian'." [9]

But Mary's great hand also recalls a typical gesture of the Theotokos when she intercedes before the Pantocrator, as happens, for example, in the Deesis and in

Marian icons of the type known as "Calcopatria" or "Haghioritisa" which depict the Virgin with her arms raised in a gesture of supplication. Mary, as Mother of God and co-operator with Christ in the work of the Redemption can intercede with her Son to help us to achieve salvation in our everyday needs, as stated by the 2nd Vatican Council (LG, 66).

7. OUR MOTHER OF PERPETUAL HELP

It is this that makes Mary the Perpetual Help of all people and this is what lies behind the title that began to be applied to the icon in the church of San Matteo in Merulana. Her hands guide us, showing us the way to Christ; they act as a gesture of intercession and supplication for the brothers and sisters of Jesus, who are also her children. This now classic passage of the 2nd Vatican Council from the Dogmatic Constitution on the Church explains this as follows:

"The motherhood of Mary in the order of grace continues without interruption from the consent which she loyally gave at the Annunciation and which she sustained without wavering beneath the cross, until the eternal consummation of all the elect. Taken up to heaven she did not lay aside this saving office but by her manifold intercession continues to procure for us the gifts of eternal salvation. By her motherly love she cares for her Son's sisters and brothers who still journey on earth surrounded by dangers and difficulties,

The eyes of the Mother look towards us with compassion and love.

until they are led into their blessed home. Therefore the blessed Virgin is invoked in the church under the titles of Advocate, Helper, Benefactress, and Mediatrix." (LG, 62).

8. THE GREAT MYSTERY OF SALVATION IN CHRIST

However, more than a specific truth of Christian dogma, the icon of Our Mother of Perpetual Help represents the mystery of Salvation in Christ. The gilded background of the icon (purest light) and the circular halos invite us to contemplate Christ and the Mother of God already living the full glory of the great mystery of the Redemption. This starts at the Incarnation and includes the "elevation" of Christ on the cross and his "ascent" into heaven on the day of the Resurrection: raised on the cross he will appear to all as the Saviour of the world; exalted at the right hand of the Father, in glory, he will send forth the Holy Spirit and through him he will extend his dominion in the world. This is why the archangels appear to repeat the following words, found on crosses of Russian origin: "We bow before the Cross and glorify your Resurrection".

The eyes of the child look resolutely and calmly towards the instrument of salvation.

Given the narrative elements of the composition, it is possible to say that Christ lives the attitude shown at his Presentation in the Temple (Lk 2:22-40) and that recalled in the letter to the Hebrews 10:5-7, which says: "You who wanted no sacrifice or oblation, prepared a body for me. You took no pleasure in holocausts or sacrifices for sin; then I said, just as I was commanded in the scroll of the book, 'God here I am! I am coming to obey your will'."

Mary's attitude recalls her words in Nazareth, "You see before you the Lord's servant, let it happen to me as you have said" (Lk 1:38) and those of the aged Simeon in the temple, "And a sword will pierce your soul too" (Lk 2:35).[10] Both these attitudes culminate in the Passion and Death of Christ. The disciple John describes these in his gospel when he refers to Mary's presence at the foot of the Cross (Jn 19:25).

Icons of the 'Virgin of the Passion' recall this in a style usually derived from the Eleusa or Hodegetria type, and, less commonly, from other very different types. The inscription, characteristic of those which, like the Perpetual Help, belong to the Cretan School, highlights the portent of the Passion, the reality of his humanity and the sorrow of Christ:

"The archangel Gabriel, who before had brought tidings of great joy to the Immaculate Virgin, now presents her with the symbols of the Passion. But Jesus Christ, in mortal flesh and fearful of death, takes fright at the sight of such things."

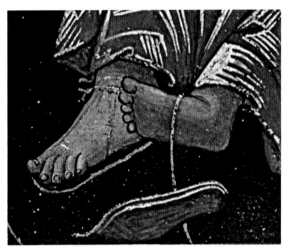

The fallen sandal that exposes the sole of Christ's right foot may signify the same fright. On the other hand this may be a subtle reference to the Book of Ruth where the sandal is described as a symbol of redemption (Ruth 4:7). Some icons that do not belong precisely to the Virgin of the Passion type, show the marks of the nails.

Symbolically, the sandal falls from the child's foot.

Mary shares in this sorrow, which is also the sorrow of the brothers and sisters of Christ and makes it her own, transfiguring it in prayer, as can be seen from her face and hands. With her hands she holds the hands of Christ, supporting he who sustains the whole world. The child, who embraces his Mother, is the Consolation and the merciful Saviour; he leans towards this creature of his own creation, seeking to console and be consoled. An eastern saint, St Sergius, expresses it thus, "When I am sad, the Mother of God weeps with me. When my soul is joyful, the Mother of God smiles with me. When I feel myself a sinner, the Mother of God intercedes on my behalf".

But if we remember the iconographic origin of *"the angels with the instruments of Calvary"* in the Virgin of the Passion theme of Cretan origin, the composition may also recall the mystery of the Resurrection of the Lord: this is what they signified in other artistic compositions in which they appeared in this manner.

And then, the Marian antiphony of Easter takes on its full meaning for the icon of Perpetual Help:

"Queen of heaven, rejoice, alleluia, for the Lord, whom you were worthy to bear, alleluia, has risen as he said, alleluia. Pray for us to God, alleluia."

In fact, what the Lord had warned the Virgin about in the dialogue by Romanus Melodos has come to pass:

"Mother, consider my death as a dream. After spending three days willingly in the tomb you will see me rise again and renew the earth and all who dwell thereon. Mother, tell these things to all and take joy in them."

This is also what St Andrew of Crete sang in the *Great Penitential Canon*, Ode IV, third canto, 18, alluding to Lk 23:42-43: "Today you will be with me in paradise".

"The Creator came down to earth to save us. He chose to be nailed to the tree of sorrows to win back for us the Paradise we had lost.
Therefore, heaven and earth, the whole of creation and the multitude of those redeemed from all the nations, do all adore you."

And the ode concludes with this Theotokion:

"You conceive, yet are a Virgin; you will remain a Virgin always because the child born of you will rewrite the laws of nature in accordance with God's will."

To truly comprehend the richness of the icon of Our Mother of Perpetual Help we must do more than give it a simply vague or even pious look. We need to tune in to the theological message it holds through an iconographic, aesthetic and spiritual 'reading' of the symbolic elements it employs. This has been our purpose in writing this book. Now, as it draws to an end we remember the words of a saint who prayed before an image of Mary every day and who hoped eventually to be able to see her not as an icon but face to face:

"Devout reader, if by chance my humble work should please you, as I hope it will, I entreat you to commend me to the Most Holy Virgin that I might find great confidence in her protection...

And farewell! Until we meet again in paradise at the feet of this most gentle Mother and her most loving Son, there to praise them, to give them thanks and to give our love to them both, face to face, for all eternity. Amen."

(St Alphonsus M. de Liguori, *The Glories of Mary.*)

The Church and Monastery of Sant' Alfonso on the Via Merulana, Rome.

Notes to Chapter V

[1] A. Grabar: *Le vie della creazione nell'iconografia cristiana: Antichità e medioevo*, Milan, 1988.

[2] From the earliest times the Blessed Virgin has been honoured with the title of "Mother of God", under whose protection the faithful take refuge together in prayer in all their perils and needs. Accordingly, especially after the Council of Ephesus, the devotion of the people of God for Mary developed enormously in veneration and love, in invocation and imitation, according to her own prophetic words: "All generations will call me blessed, because he who is mighty has done great things to me" (Lk 1:48-49). Vatican Council II, LG 66.

[3] cf. Ch. II.

[4] For a theological reading of the Pantocrator, cf. Rom 8:29; 1 Cor 15:49; Eph 1:1-2,10; Phil 2:6-11; Col 1:15-20; Heb 1:3, and others.

[5] I. Gebara-M. C. Lucchetti Bingemer: *María*, in I. Ellacuría-J. Sobrino: *Mysterium liberationis. Conceptos fundamentales de la teología de la liberación*, I, Madrid, 1990, 609.

[6] Gebara-Lucchetti Bingemer, 609.

[7] Grabar, 163.

[8] Grabar, 164.

[9] Secretariado of the C. E. de Seminarios y Universidades-Secretariado de Vocaciones de la Confer. *María dijo 'sí'. María y la vocación en la Iglesia.* Madrid, 1988, 23-24. cf. J. A. Domínguez Asensio, *María, estrella de la Evangelización, Madre de Dios y nuestra*, Madrid, 1991.

[10] Origenes, *Comentario al Evangelio de Lucas,* Rome, 1974, 133.

The Shrine of Our Mother of Perpetual Help in Singapore is renowned as the great centre of devotion. Here we see the wonderfully decorated Shrine, bedecked with flowers for the Jubilee Year 2000, celebrating Mary's "Yes".

Appendix I

THE ST MATTHEW BOARD IN MERULANA

T his document relates to the provenance of the icon of Our Mother of Perpetual Help and to the beginning of its veneration in the church of S. Matteo in Merulana, Rome, at the end of the 15th century. The text was translated from Latin by T. Cepedal. It quotes from the wording on a small board placed in front of the altar on which the icon was displayed. The text relates 'how the image of the Virgin Mary was moved to this church of St Matthew the Apostle'. For the original text and other related texts, cf. F. Ferrero, *Nuestra Senora del Perpetuo Socorro* , Madrid, 1966.

The Church and Convent of St Matthew on the Via Merulana, 18th century engraving.
This was the home of the icon of Our Mother of Perpetual Help for three hundred years,
until it was demolished in 1798.

"How the image of the Virgin Mary was moved to this church of St Matthew the Apostle:

A certain merchant stole this image of the Virgin from his homeland of Crete, where, in a church on that same island, it had produced many miracles. He concealed the image among his baggage and leaving that place embarked on a ship. A fearful storm arose, of such ferocity that the passengers despaired of their salvation and, unaware of the image, made many vows to God and to the Virgin entreating them to free them from this imminent danger.

Through divine providence they reached their port of destination. A year later the merchant arrived in Rome, bringing the image with him. Later a serious illness afflicted him and he made contact with a certain friend in Rome, asking him to care for him in his sickness and promising to reward him for this if God should see fit to return him to health. The Roman friend brought him to his home and attended him with great care. His illness grew worse and, realising that his final hour was near, he summoned his friend and, with tears in his eyes, asked him to grant him one last favour. The Roman promised him this.

The merchant then revealed the whole story of the image, how he had stolen it from a church where it had been producing miracles and that this image was among his belongings.

"I therefore entreat you," he added, "now that my imminent death prevents me from taking it to the place I intended, to bring it to the church most fitting for the image". Once the merchant was dead and the image had been found among his belongings, the Roman's wife, after much pleading, succeeded in keeping the image in the house and had it in her bed chamber for nine months. The glorious Virgin admonished the Roman in a vision, urging him not to keep the image but to take it to a more suitable place. He, however, paid no heed.

After some time, the Virgin returned to admonish him for keeping the image in his house. Again he disobeyed her wishes and again she admonished him, adding that if it were not placed in a church he would meet a bad end. The Roman then began to take fright and when morning came he told his wife what had happened, asking her to hand the image over to a church. His wife, affecting surprise at his words, replied that she was a Christian, not a pagan and that they were not the only ones to have such images in their house; and moreover that no Christian, no matter how sinful, would be without an image of the Virgin, of Christ on the cross, or something similar. At this the Roman conceded to his wife's wishes. Once again the Virgin appeared to him in his dreams and said to him:

"I have warned you repeatedly, even with threats, that you should take my image from this place and you have chosen not to believe me; it is clear that you must depart first if I am to find a more worthy abode."

The Roman then fell ill and died. Some time later the Virgin appeared to his six year old daughter and said to her: "Give this message to your mother and to your grandfather: Holy Mary of Perpetual Help requires that you remove her from your house, if not, you will all soon die". The girl told her mother of the vision and the mother then became fearful because she too had had the same vision; she broke into tears when she realised that she had been the cause of her husband's death and quickly took the decision to remove the image from the house.

A neighbour, seeing her in tears, asked her the reason. She told her all that had happened – her husband's vision, his death because she had not believed him and had gone against his wishes – and she grieved and lamented because her husband had died because of her.

Her neighbour replied: "You are mistaken, only fools believe such things; the Virgin Mary is in heaven and does not concern herself with what we may do with her images; if you threw it on the fire it would burn like any other piece of wood. And if you are so afraid – she added – give it to me" and continued with other disrepectful words. However, that evening, on returning home she was seized by a strange pain that was removed only after she had made a promise to the image.

Finally, the glorious Virgin appeared again to the little girl and told her to tell her mother that the image must be placed between St Mary Major and St John Lateran, in a church dedicated to the apostle Matthew. Her mother obeyed and, having advised the friars of St Augustine at this church, with the help of the clergy and all the people, the image was taken there and on the very day of its removal the first miracle occurred: an individual totally paralysed in the right arm and side was suddenly freed from his ailment after simply commending himself to God and the Virgin and making a promise.

So it was that this image of the most glorious Virgin was placed in the church of St Matthew the Apostle on 27 March 1499, the 7th year of the Pontificate of his Holiness, Father and Lord in Christ, Pope Alexander VI."

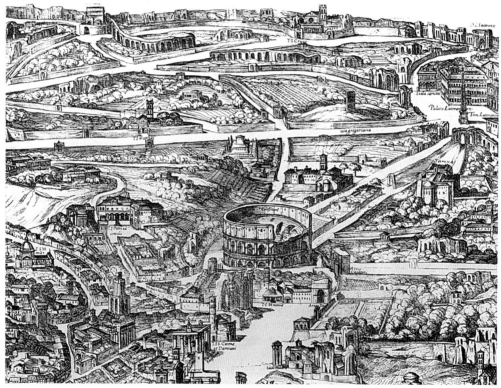

Detail from the plan of Rome in the 18th century. The Via Gregoriana (now Via Merulana) cuts across the centre. Above the Coliseum to the left can be seen the church and convent of St Matthew.

The Shrine of our Mother of Perpetual Help in Sant' Alfonso Church, Rome

The chapel of Our Lady of Lourdes where the icon was first displayed.

This altar and reredos were erected in 1871.

The shrine until the restoration of 1994.

The altar and shrine restored and redesigned in 1994.

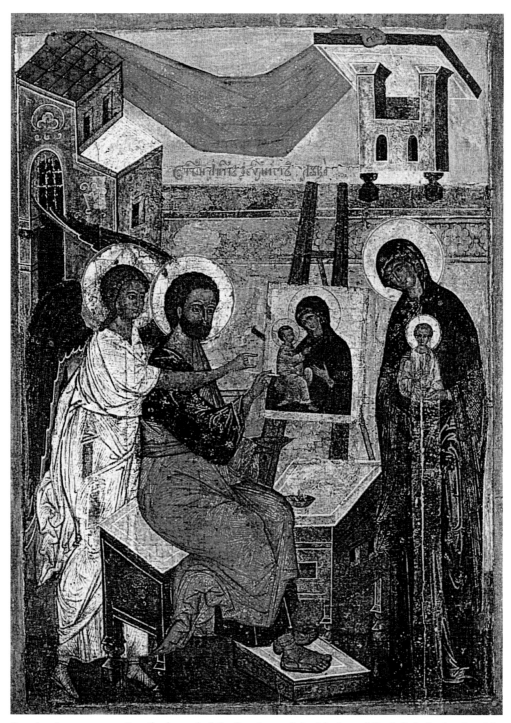

Russian icon representing the legend of the first icon of the Mother of God. St Luke (assisted by an angel) is painting the Virgin Mary.

Appendix II

ILLUSTRATIONS

I t would be impossible to illustrate in detail the entire process of Marian iconography that led to the creation of the icon of Our Mother of Perpetual Help (the icon studied here). However, we have managed to illustrate the five fundamental themes which give us a better understanding of the iconographic theme of the Virgin of the Passion, to which this icon belongs. Needless to say, we have only been able to reproduce a limited number of significant examples for each theme.

To identify icons from the Redemptorist archive in Rome, to which special attention has been given in this book and the majority of which had never before been published, we refer to:

i) Inventarium Imaginum Parvi Musaei Beatae Mariae Virginis de Perpetuo Succursu Anno Dni 1910 incoepti (cited as Inventarium). Original 16 folio manuscript by the Spanish Redemptorist Antonio Mariscal González, (28 April 1866 to 26 August 1936), preserved in the Archivum Generale Historicum Redemptoristarum (AGHR) - (PS, 1 2)

ii) Elenco delle Icone Bizantine della SS. Vergine esposte nel Pontificio Collegio Ucraino di S. Giosafat, 25 March to 2 April 1965 (cited as Elenco), folios 1 and 2, which contain the icons included here.

For more complete Iconographic Documentation and technical data for many of the illustrations we refer you to the original Spanish edition of this book, *UN ICONO DE LA SANTA MADRE DE DIOS, VIRGEN DE LA PASION*, Madrid, 1994.

Information is given with the illustrations throughout the book. Here more information is added where appropriate.

8   This photograph of the restored shrine and others of the church and shrine of Sant' Alfonso, Rome, used with permission of Fr Marek Kotynski, C.Ss.R., Shrine of Our Mother of Perpetual Help, Rome.

19 Photograph of the church of St Alphonsus Liguori, "The Rock" Church, in St Louis, MO, USA, by Fr. Rick M. Potts, C.Ss.R.

22 The Virgin of the Sign with St Nicholas and St Blaise, 15th to 16th centuries. Museum of History, Moscow, Novgorod school. The central figure of this Novgorod triptych is a reproduction of another famous 12th century icon. The presence of saints in the work of this school is characteristic of the 15th century.

35 The Madonna of Comfort, 5th century. Basilica of Santa Francesca Romana in the Forum, Rome. This comes from the Basilica of Santa Maria Antigua, 5th century. Photograph Giorgio Vasari, Rome, 1991.

37 The Virgin of Mercy, 17th century. Redemptorist archive in Rome. Photograph Giorgio Vasari, Rome, 1991. This is an example of a Virgin of the Passion of the Italo-Greek school from which only the angels are missing. They were probably on the doors of the triptych.

46 The Annunciation, 5th century. Rome, triumphal arch mosaic (432-440) at St Mary Major, originally dedicated to the Theotokos. It is a celebration of the doctrine of the Council of Ephesus (431). The representation is filled with a regal and triumphal air, as shown in the tunic, the ornaments, the Virgin's hair and the footstool on which she rests her feet.

50 The Virgin of Prompt Help, 14th century. Hodegetria known as Mater Dei velox propitia. Redemptorist archive of Rome. Photograph Giorgio Vasari, Rome, 1991. Acquired by Father De Sanctis in Cortona (Italy) in 1907 and given as a gift to the Superior General of the Redemptorists, Fr Mathias Raus (1829-1917).

The Eleusa of the Passion with angels and saints, 18th century. Casa Grande icon collection, Torrejon de Ardoz, Madrid. The faces of Mother and child are placed close together in an attitude of tenderness. However, the movements of the child's hands and feet correspond closely to those of the Virgin of the Passion type. The scroll of the angel on the right reads: "Hail, for you carry he who will save all" recalling the powerful Mother of God, the Theotokos, who carries in her arms he who can save the world and who is therefore the beginning of a spiritual regeneration.

60   The Hodegetria of Tichwin, 18th century. Redemptorist archive, Rome. Photograph Giorgi Vasari, Rome, 1991. May come from the Ukraine. Fr. Mariscal calls it the B.M.V. Smolenskaja and says of it: "The Reverend Father P. Garenaux found this image in the attic of our Bishop Eton house in England and sent it to Astorga [Leon, Spain] to Father Mariscal who in turn took it with him to Rome. Reverend Father Howel recognised the image and related how a Russian priest, who did not stay in the congregation, had bought it for fifty francs in an antique shop in London".

65   Our Lady of Grace, 16th century, Redemptorist archive, Rome. Photograph Giorgio Vasari, Rome 1991.

70   The Eleusa of the Passion, 16th century. Redemptorist archive in Rome. Photograph Giorgio Vasari, Rome, 1991. In this icon, the outstanding features are the proximity of the faces and the hands and the presentation of the sole of the foot. The infant Jesus also holds a rolled scroll in his right hand (resting on his knees), while with his left hand he clasps the Virgin's right hand. This iconographic theme is also addressed by Andrea Rizo of Candia in his own style.

78   The Virgin of the Passion, 17th century. Redemptorist archive in Rome. Photograph Giorgio Vasari, Rome, 1991. The image had been in the Redemptorist Generalate House from the time of Father Mauron. "A lady gave it as a gift to Father Berthe in Boulogne-Sur-Mer and he sent it to Father Mauron. In 1909, when it was found by Father Mariscal, it was deemed to be of great interest for studies on the Virgin of Perpetual Help".

84   Our Mother of Perpetual Help, 17th to 18th centuries. Redemptorist archive in Rome. Photograph Giorgio Vasari, Rome, 1991. This appears to be a copy of the icon of Our Mother of Perpetual Help, although with some variants. There is no background gilding. The gilded halo, with its unusual decoration, and star therefore stand out. The colours too are different. This image owes its importance to the fact that it is a pre-1866 copy of the Roman icon. This enables us to interpret photographs prior to the restoration more accurately and to judge their validity.

100 Our Mother of Perpetual Help. Black and white photograph prior to restoration of the icon. This was completed by 15 March 1866. In the General Historical

Archive of the Redemptorists in Rome, there are three photographs the same as this although with different shades of colouring. Another was used in a montage to superimpose the crown. A copy of this is also preserved. The reproduction here is based on a photograph of the original executed by Dr. Giorgio Vasari, Rome, 1991.

111 Copy of the icon of Our Mother of Perpetual Help. Redemptorist archive in Rome. Photograph Giorgio Vasari, Rome, 1991. This image was given to Pope Pius IX as a gift by Father Nicolas Mauron, the Redemptorist Superior General, on 21 April 1866. On the reverse side in black capital letters are the words: 'J. Wuger Helvet, Cop. 1866'. This is a copy of the icon as it appeared before the addition of the crowns.

113 Photograph of the Shrine of Our Mother of Perpetual Help in "The Rock" Church, St Louis, MO, USA, by Fr. Rick M. Potts, C.Ss.R.

115 Stained glass window from Kansas City, MO, USA, photograph by Fr. Rick M. Potts, C.Ss.R.

130 Photograph of the Novena celebrations in Singapore (also pp. 15 and 27) from The Sowers, Novena Church, Singapore, and Brother Bernard Heaney, C.Ss.R.

Appendix III

SHRINES OF OUR MOTHER OF PERPETUAL HELP AROUND THE WORLD

Italy
Santuario Madonna del Perpetuo Soccoro, Chiesa di S. Alfonso,
    Via Merulana, 31, I-00185 Roma

Argentina
Parroquia N.S. del Perpetuo Socorro, Av. Alberdi 580, S 2000 EON Rosario (Santa Fe)

Australia
Redemptorists, 68 Woodstock St., Mayfield, NSW 2304

Redemptorists, 190 Vincent St., North Perth, WA 6006

Austria
Maria am Gestade, Salvatorgasse 12, A-1010, Wien

Maria Puchheim, Gmundnerstrasse 3, A-4800 Attnang-Puchheim

Redemptoristenkolleg, Wichtelgasse 74, A-1170, Wien-Hernals

Bolivia
Centro Perpetuo Socorro, Casilla 146, Oruro

Brasil
Pedro Juan Caballero, Perpetuo Socorro, Caixa Postal 20, 79900-000 Ponta Pora – MS

Paróquia Nª Sª Perpétuo Socorro, C.P. 11122, 05422-970 São Paulo - SP

Nª Sª Perpétuo Socorro Bodocongó, C.P. 282, 58100-970 Campina Grande - PB

Paróquia Nª Sª Perpétuo Socorro, Caixa Postal 236, 55293-970 Garanhuns - PE

Santuário Nª Sª do Perp. Socorro, C.P. 114.277, 28001-970 Campos - RJ

Igreja Nª Sª do Perpétuo Socorro, C.P. 4010, 66113-970 Belém - PA

Santuário N. S. Perpétuo Socorro, C.P. 2001, 79005-001 Campo Grande - MS

Paróquia Nª Sª Perpétuo Socorro, C.P. 20013, 80062-990 Curitiba - PR

Paróquia Nª Sª Perpétuo Socorro, C.P. 10506, 71620-908 Brasilia - CF

Burkina Faso
Perpetual Help, Mission Catholique, B.P. 204 Diabo, Burkina Faso

Canada
Perpetual Help Residence, 426 St. Germain Ave., Toronto, ON M5M 1W7

St Patrick's, 141 McCall Street, Totonto, On, M5T 1W3

O.L.P.H. Rectory, 2465 Crown Street, Vancouver, BC, V6R 3V9

Chile
Parroquia Nª Sª del Perp. Socorro, Casilla 47, Correo 2, Santiago
Parr. Nª Sª del Perpetuo Socorro, Casilla 568, Temuco
Parr. Nª Sª del Perpetuo Socorro, Casilla 13, Valparaiso

Colombia
Parroquia Perpetuo Socorro, Carrera 46 Nº 66-33, Barranquilla (Atlántico)
Parroquia Perpetuo Socorro, Carrera 17 Nº 51-05, Bucaramanga, (Santander Sur)
Parroquia Nª Sª del Perpetuo Socorro, Carrera 23, Nº 5-74, Popayán, (Cauca)

Ecuador
Santuario del Perpetuo Socorro, Apartado 4903, Manta

England
St Mary's, Clapham Park Road, Clapham, London SW4 7AP
Erdington Abbey, Sutton Road, Birmingham, B23 6QN
Our Lady of the Annunciation, Bishop Eton, Woolton Road, Liverpool, L16 8NQ

Germany
Redemptoristen-Kloster, Ludwigstrasse 16, D-93413 Cham/Opf
Redemptoristenkloster Maria Hilf, Klosterstrasse 30, D-44787 Bochum

Honduras
Parroqia Nª Sª Perpetuo Socorro, Trojes, Dpto. El Paraiso

India
Our Lady of Perpetual Help Church, St Anthony's Road, Chembur, Mumbai 400 071

Ireland
Clonard Monastery, 1 Clonard Gardens, Falls Road, Belfast BT13 2RL
Mount St Alphonsus, Henry Street, S.C.R., Limerick

Lebanon
Ecole N.D. du Perpétuel Secours, P.O. Box 90713, Jdeidet-el-Metn

Mexico
Iglesia del Perpetuo Socorro, Tomasa Estévez, 405, 78250 San Luis Potosi

Paraquay
Perpetuo Socorro, Casilla Correo 665, Asunción

Peru
Parroquia Virgen del Perp. Socorro, Apartado 32, Alto San Martin (Arequipa), Mariano Melgar
Parroquia Perpetuo Socorro, Apartado 224, Lima 100

Philippines
Perpetual Help Shrine, Baclaran, Parañaque, 1700 Metro Manila
Perpetual Help Parish, P.O. Box 139, 6200 Dumaguete City
Perpetual Help Parish, P.O. Box 143, 6500 Tacloban City

Portugal
Perpetuo Socorro, Rua da Firmeza, 161-163, P-4000-228 Porto

Scotland
St Mary's, Hatton Road, Kinnoull, Perth PH2 7BP

Singapore
Novena Church, 300 Thomson Road, Singapore 307653

South Africa
St Mary's, Retreat Road, 7945 Retreat

Spain
Perpetuo Socorro, Manuel Silvela 14, E-28010 Madrid
Parroquia del Perpetuo Socorro, Avda. Soleá, 17, E-11404 Jerez de la Frontera (Cádiz)
Perpetuo Socorro, Lalin, 3, E-36209 Vigo (Pontevedra)

Thailand
Holy Redeemer, 123/19 Ruam Rudee Lane 5, Bangkok 10330

United States of America
Mission Church Rectory, 1545 Tremont Street, Boston, MA 02120-2996
Perpetual Help Center, 294 East 150th Street, Bronx, NY 10451-5195
O.L.P.H. Rectory, 526 – 59th Street, Brooklyn, NY 11220-3899
O.L.P.H. Rectory, 323 East 61st Street, New York, NY 10021-8703
O.L.P.H. Retreat and Spirituality Center, 3989 South Moon Drive, Venice, FL 34292
Our Lady of Perpetual Help Rectory, 3333 Broadway, Kansas City, MO 64111-2498
St Alphonsus Rectory, 1118 N. Grand Blvd, Saint Louis, MO 63106
O.L.P.H. Parish, 618 South Grimes Street, San Antonio, TX 78203-2144

Venezuela
Parr. Nª Sª del Perpetuo Socorro, Carrera 12, n° 12-32, San Cristobal (Táchira) 5001

Zimbabwe
The Redemptorists, Alphonsus House, P.O. Box 30, Tafara, Harare